The Shortest Distance Between You and Your New Product

HOW INNOVATORS USE RAPID
LEARNING CYCLES TO GET THEIR BEST
IDEAS TO MARKET FASTER

Katherine Radeka

2nd Edition

Chesapeake Research Press
Camas, Washington, USA

You may use the work for your own noncommercial and personal use; any other use of the work is strictly prohibited. Your right to use the work may be terminated if you fail to comply with these terms.

Table of Contents

To all of the innovators who seek better solutions to the world's most important challenges.

Get Your Best Ideas to Market Faster

This book will help you find the shortest distance between you and a new product* that your customers can buy. It is about how to bring your new product vision to life, as quickly as possible, while holding true to the essential element of the vision: the value that you strive to create for your customers.

Bring Ideas to Life

A new idea becomes an innovation when it's been turned into a product that delivers the value that it promises. Until then, it's just an idea.

Solo entrepreneurs, startups and established R&D groups look different from one another, but they all share the goal of turning ideas into winning products, as rapidly as possible.

---

* For simplicity, I use "product" to encompass new software, business models, processes and services as well as tangible products. "Product development" is the process of turning an idea into a product.

This requires some kind of product development process. Established companies often have elaborate Product Development Processes (PDPs) with templates, checklists, management reviews and even audits. These processes are fine for incremental improvements to existing product lines, but they often break down in the face of a truly novel idea. They don't support innovation.

A solo entrepreneur or a young startup team may have no process at all. An entrepreneur's development process can be a simple one: experiment with it until it works. If the entrepreneur is self-funded, this process can continue indefinitely. But most products require more funding than the entrepreneur has to invest, and at some point outside investors want to see something that works, as well as paying customers who are satisfied.

There is no "cookbook" method or standard process to go from idea to product launch. Over the years, a lot of people have tried to create one, with varying degrees of success. All of them work well in some situations, but not so well in others. Every innovation needs to overcome specific challenges, but the challenges are never the same.

This book proposes a framework to structure the work you need to do to overcome your idea's specific obstacles. The framework is highly adaptable to meet the conditions you face. Unlike standard procedures, it minimizes the number of mandatory steps to the critical few that you need to organize your team's activities. At every step, the specific actions you take will depend entirely upon the needs of your development program.

If it's more comfortable, you can use this framework as a procedure, by following the steps exactly as I've laid them out in the book. But I suspect that many of you will absorb the ideas in this book and then use them as the basis for developing your own process—which may be different for every product you bring to market.

Don't Break the Rules—Make Your Own

Innovation teams often get told that the rules don't apply to them. You can't read *Fast Company*, visit an innovation group on LinkedIn or view many blog posts before you trip over the admonition, "Break all the rules!"

I understand where that comes from. I worked on some early e-commerce applications, back when we were still trying to figure out how to get people to push the "Buy" button, and we were burdened with a heavyweight waterfall software development process that was not working for us at all.

There is nothing more frustrating than burning with the vision for a new product, a new business, a new work of art only to be told that it can't be done the way you want to do it, yet knowing that it can't be done the way they want you to do it. Something has to give, and if you're as driven as I am, it's the process that breaks, damn the consequences.

I've been on the other side, too—the place where there are no rules at all. Before I started college, I spent a year developing a database for a research lab at Baylor College of Medicine. I knew nothing about software development—and I was the only one in the lab who could even turn on the computer until I trained an assistant. Then I worked my way through college by developing and maintaining a system to estimate and generate proposals for a local construction company. I was an IT department of one, accountable to nobody. I just hacked something together and then taught people how to use it.

It all started in my freshman year, when I was hired as a word processor to type client estimates. I built a primitive spreadsheet for myself, so that I would not have to do as much manual work to check the math on the proposals that my boss generated by hand. By the time I was a senior, the system had grown into a database-driven application with a user interface that was easy enough for the project manager to use, even though this was the first software he had ever used.

It was an incredible learning experience and makes a great story, but the truth is that it was so much more painful than it had to be. It just wasn't good enough to turn into a product that I could sell to other construction companies.

It was too finicky and required too much babysitting. I needed to stay on call to support that company for three years after I graduated, until they replaced it with commercial estimation software. No one else could maintain it. It was too highly optimized for the company owner's personal estimation process to adapt for other types of projects. If I had tried to turn that software into a product, it would have failed quickly, for reasons that I could have prevented if I'd only followed a few simple guidelines for product design and development—a framework, not a procedure.

The Rapid Learning Cycles Framework

The Rapid Learning Cycles framework addresses the one big obstacle that everyone encounters in product development sooner or later.

Product development, the way most people do it, is one long, slow learning loop. In early development, we make decisions to lock down requirements and demonstrate feasibility, so that we can get the funding to move into development. Or we hack away at our good idea until we get something that seems to work, at least in the garage.

Our default mode is Build–Test–Fix. This is the way we learned to do things in school, where our homework assignments consisted of discrete tasks that built on each other in a predesigned sequence. Even I will fall into this pattern if I'm doing something that looks like it's easy, and even I fail to recognize that I've gotten stuck in Build–Test–Fix when a task is not as simple as it looks. But the solutions we come up with in Build–Test–Fix mode are the first ones we happen to find, and not the best ones. They often come with hidden problems that we won't find until later.

Then later, when things don't work out as expected, we revisit our decisions. We loop back to redo things that we thought we had finished. In the worst case, we don't learn until after the product has been released and customers complain—or refuse to buy the product at all.

The path from idea to launch careens from problem to problem, backing up, retracing steps and trying random new directions. Finally, the product is good enough or the group decides to ship with what they have, the project gets canceled or the business runs out of money. The original innovator is often frustrated that the final product does not realize the original vision.

These long, slow learning cycles have implications that directly affect our ability to realize our vision for a new product:

- Inability to release a product on schedule that allows our sales and marketing partners to do their best work
- Slow time to market, with a long time to recoup investment costs or earn money to invest in future innovations
- Overloaded resources, making it hard to staff up new projects for success or make good decisions on prioritizing features
- Quality problems that escape into Operations and sometimes out to the customer
- Increased costs throughout the product's lifecycle, from development through obsolescence
- Business partners who lack confidence that the product development organization can deliver

The way to fix long, slow learning cycles is to break them apart and speed them up.

We transform them into Rapid Learning Cycles.

Rapid Learning Cycles Speed Up Product Development

Rapid Learning Cycles are synchronized sets of experiments to remove uncertainty, manage risk and build knowledge before key decisions need to be made within a product development program.

Allen Ward of the University of Michigan first described Rapid Learning Cycles in his book *The LPD Skills Kit,* which he published in a limited edition for his clients in 2003. He based his work partially on his studies of the process for evaluating wing designs in wind tunnels.

When the Wright Brothers set out to build an airplane, they knew that if their design had any flaws, their test pilot may not survive to make a second attempt. It had to be right the first time. They conducted a series of modeling experiments to learn how to design the wings and the controls so that the airplane could take off—and land—from the very first flight.

Ward had a theoretical understanding of Rapid Learning Cycles but had not seen any examples of them. He had seen enough to know that traditional project management didn't work very well in product development. A military veteran, he wrote about "combat planning" as a model for dealing with uncertainty. But he didn't know about the body of knowledge that Agile Software Development experts had been developing to overcome the same obstacles.

It took a few people who had solid grounding in Agile Development, like Tim Schipper at Steelcase and Kathy Iberle at Hewlett Packard, to put the pieces together. In the last six years, this has been the primary focus of my work.

The results have been outstanding: products launched months earlier than expected, products that exceeded expectations for delivering customer and business value, joint development with customers to shave years off the total time to market.

My biggest satisfaction has come from teams that use Rapid Learning Cycles to pursue ideas that would be too risky with a traditional approach to development. Rapid Learning Cycles have helped these teams demonstrate that their idea is a good one, and eliminate the risks that made their investors or managers squeamish.

When we combine the Wright Brothers' approach to experimentation with Agile project management practices, we get a repeatable framework that you can use to help your product development teams release innovative products that your company may not have had the courage to pursue before.

Rapid Learning Cycles Extend Agile Development to All Types of Products

Agile Software Development is built around rapid cycles of feedback: go a short distance toward the goal, and then check in with everyone—especially the customer—to make sure we're still going in the right direction. In the meantime, make the work visible and give others (customers and managers) specific points in the process when they can intervene, leaving the team free to work the rest of the time.

This is easy to do in software. You can apply code changes and test them immediately. You can automate the core tests to make regression testing fast and reliable. You can easily build test harnesses and simulations for the parts of the system that aren't built yet. You can push rapid iteration so far that you have daily integration, letting developers know right away if they have introduced a problem into the design.

In the hardware world, things are not so easy, for three reasons:

- **CAD tools, simulation modeling, 3D printing and other rapid prototyping tools have definitely come a long way,** but physical, chemical and biological products still require real-world testing that takes time.

- **Small-scale prototypes and small lot sizes don't always accurately predict performance** when the product is produced at full scale, and the product must meet the demands of the manufacturing process. Fully functional prototypes and full-scale process runs are expensive and take a long time to set up.

- **Most products these days are not manufactured where they are designed.** Instead, complex networks of vendors form "supply chains" that feed the final assembly lines. These suppliers can be anywhere in the world. This may be the most efficient way to manufacture a product, but it slows down development because it requires so much coordination across company and geographic boundaries.

An Agile Software Development team learns through building the product. For the most part, they use a set of well-known technologies (coding languages, algorithms, protocols) and an established technology platform (the chip, the operating system, the Internet.)

The authors of the Agile Manifesto saw that fast cycles of Build–Test–Fix were the best way to understand what users need, since few users can give good feedback on something they have not seen. But most innovation programs have deeper questions to answer than that.

While the Agile method is good for answering questions about functionality and user interfaces in software, it breaks down when a provisional architecture isn't good enough to support a breakthrough technology. The method says nothing about how to answer questions related to the regulatory landscape or channel partners. The cost of a Build–Test–Fix cycle in software is the cost of the developers' time. In hardware, we need to coordinate with the model shop, suppliers and testing groups, all of whom have other programs competing for their time.

This is why Agile Development is not enough on its own. You can speed up these Build–Test–Fix cycles and get your product to market faster than you would if you made a rigid project plan and tried to deliver too much in your first release.

But you will still waste a lot of time and money, and your customers and investors will still wait for the product a lot longer than they need to. Your product may still be plagued with late design loopbacks that cause delays or feature reductions. And your customers may still not like the product that you release—not because the idea is bad, but because the execution is poorly done.

You can improve this model by using a few ideas from Eric Ries's book *The Lean Startup*. Ries refines Build–Test–Fix into Build–Measure–Learn, which at least ensures that you are getting measurable results from your cycles. He also describes the Minimum Viable Product (MVP), the smallest product you can release to real customers to enable one full turn of Build–Measure–Learn.

This is a useful concept when you are ready, but usually, you have faster, cheaper and easier ways to learn about your customers, technology and business models before you need to build an MVP.

If you rush into Build–Test–Fix or Build–Measure–Learn, you will run the maze faster, but you will still run the maze—not cut through it.

Cut Through the Maze of the Fuzzy Front End

What if you could float a maze to see all the blind alleys, wrong turns and dead ends before you started? What if you could see exactly which walls to remove in order to cut a straight path through the maze?

With Rapid Learning Cycles, you will seek that path, with the fastest, easiest, quickest tools you have available to you. You will remove the walls. Once you've built the straight road, there is nothing that stands between you and your new product.

When you finish reading this book, you will have enough information to use the Rapid Learning Cycles framework on your next development project.

- If you are an entrepreneur, this will help you turn your idea into a great product—or learn quickly if your idea has some major problems that cannot be overcome before you've spent three years of your life on it.
- If you are an R&D manager, you will be able to run your next development project with Rapid Learning Cycles, and you will know how to work within your company's PDP to use them. You will be able to use some of the concepts no matter where you are in a project that is already past early development.
- If you are an R&D leader, you will understand why products take so long to get to market in your existing structure, and what changes to make in order to get all of your products to market faster.

The shortest distance between you and your new product is a series of Rapid Learning Cycles.

PART ONE

The Shortest Distance Between You and Your Product

CHAPTER ONE

Why Rapid Learning Cycles?

I n most places, the work to turn an idea into a product consists of one long, slow learning cycle. It's as if we go from San Francisco to Los Angeles by way of New York.

I've been a developer of one kind or another since my first job out of high school. I loved seeing my companies' products—the ones I worked on and my clients' products—get out into the world.

I have bittersweet memories of all-night debugging sessions, last-minute product changes and launch celebrations where we were all too tired to party. I've watched product ideas bounce up and down the priority list. I've seen my projects suffer from last-minute travel restrictions or budget cuts. I've been on the receiving end of phone calls from executives demanding to know why a product would miss its launch date.

Most of the time, the pain was worth the joy of seeing the product on the shelf. But it takes a heavy toll on people. I dedicated the last twelve years of my life to getting the fun and excitement back into product development—to minimize the pain and maximize the joy.

In the last six years, I have worked with world-leading companies to develop a much better way to do product development that is more joyful and less frustrating. Together, we have figured out how to eliminate those long, slow learning cycles.

Long, Slow Learning Cycles Get in the Way

In most product development programs, we try to run as fast as possible, but our efforts slow everything down.

Our assumptions about development, our eagerness to bring our new idea to life and established Product Development Processes drive us to make decisions early in development. The only information we have to go on when making these decisions is our past experience and our vision for the product. Later, when things don't work out the way we expected, we have to revisit those decisions. In the worst case, we don't learn until after the product has been released and customers complain—or refuse to buy the product at all. We spend too much time on the wrong ideas, while our best ideas suffer from poor execution.

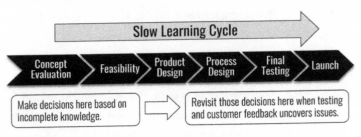

Figure 1.1: Most Product Development Is One Long Slow Learning Cycle

These long, slow learning cycles directly affect the success of our products. When we make decisions too early, we end up in redesign loopbacks to fix problems that crop up, or we release the product without fixing them and suffer the consequences. Sometimes groups try to eliminate the redesign work by locking down decisions even earlier—but that doesn't work. It just makes the learning cycles longer, because even less information is available to inform the initial decisions.

What if you went on a hike to the top of Dog Mountain but realized after fifteen minutes that you left your car unlocked, and you had to return to the trailhead? Then, an hour later, you found out that you left your camera at the creek ten minutes back? Then chose the wrong path at a confusing trail crossing? All of these require us to loop back to an earlier place in the hike. These loopbacks slow our progress, and could keep us from reaching the top at all if we want to finish by nightfall. When we do reach the top, we may be too tired to enjoy it.

Loopbacks plague product developers working in both startup organizations and long-established companies. In a startup, the passion of the product vision, the push to earn revenue before the money runs out and investors lose patience, and the natural optimism it takes to be entrepreneurs combine to build pressure to move quickly without taking any time for investigation. Teams just dive in and start building stuff using whatever tools are at hand, and whatever people are willing to take the risk.

In an established company, the product development process can be so risk-averse that great ideas have to jump through a lot of hoops to get funded. This forces decisions that the team isn't ready to make, in order to build a business case that will support the product's investment. Once an idea gets in the portfolio, it becomes difficult to kill—even if it's clear that the product will not achieve its goals. Finally, companies tend to stuff their portfolios with too many projects, so that every project team is starved for resources and driven to take shortcuts.

In any company, the pressure is to make decisions fast and early, deferring learning until later, if at all. Intuitively, this makes sense: the best way to learn how to build a product is to build the product.

The Pressure to Build the Product Quickly Slows the Product Down

If we had perfect knowledge of the work to be done to get from here to there, it would make sense to dive in and build. We could make decisions early and then hold people accountable for executing them flawlessly. But that's not how innovation works. If we already know how to do something, it's not innovation.

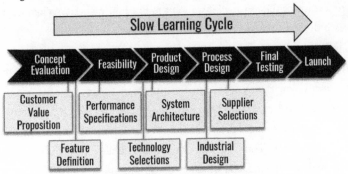

Figure 1.2: A Few of the Sources of Long, Slow Learning Cycles

I once asked a group of product development managers to draw their Product Development Process (PDP) for me. It looked like a long, winding path with uncrossable rivers, blind canyons and unexpected cliffs. The development teams were running as fast as they could toward their goal, but managers (the people making the drawing) were constantly throwing rocks in their way. Meanwhile, the team spent a lot of time building bridges over the widest spots in the river, setting up rappel lines to get down those cliff walls and backtracking out of blind canyons.

In the physical world, the journey with the shortest travel time is rarely a straight line. You can hack your way through the wilderness by following a compass, but that wastes a lot of energy. To find the best route, you need to understand the lay of the land: the natural mountain passes, the animal trails that naturally follow the terrain and the spots in the river that are easiest to cross. It takes a little extra time and patience, but it saves so much more than it costs.

The Drive to Make Quick Decisions Wastes Time

When decisions come early and learning comes late, you've headed off on a compass direction without understanding the terrain. A lot of unnecessary obstacles get in the way between you and your new product:

- **It takes a long time to move from a good concept to a profitable product that meets customer expectations.** The group gets stuck in a long series of Build–Test–Fix loops. Unanticipated problems that don't have easy fixes tend to pop up during the late phases of development. Launch dates slip, and market windows get missed. Investors get impatient with a team that's stuck in "almost done." Lead customers, who may have helped you design the product, get nervous when they can't meet their own internal milestones.

- **It takes a long time to learn whether or not the idea is fundamentally flawed, and therefore should have been stopped sooner.** The company wastes money on ideas that should have been killed a lot earlier, and the innovators spend too much of their lives working on unsuccessful products that they could have spent investigating new product opportunities.

- **The end product is disappointing.** The execution is not nearly as smooth or well designed as the innovators envisioned. The product may be slower than expected, unreliable, difficult to scale to sufficient volume or clunky in a way that even early customers won't accept. This erodes profitability with low yields, scrap and warranty returns, and erodes customer confidence. The problems may even require expensive and embarrassing recalls that kill all the profits from the product.

- **The product costs more, from idea through obsolescence.** The drive to "make it work" leads to solutions that add cost to the product at the end, and those costs stay with the product throughout its life. It may be difficult to maintain, difficult to service and even difficult to recycle at the end.

- **Business partners and customers lose confidence in the development team's ability to deliver.** Failure to meet promised milestones, business cases that show less and less profitability and constantly slipping launch dates erode trust. The delays make it a lot more difficult for your investors, lead customers and partners to support you when the product is ready for launch.

- **Once your product ships, you have nowhere to go next.** You've just learned a lot, but that knowledge is not extensible into the next product in the product family. The developers know only about the decisions they made that worked or didn't work for this product. They know nothing about how to meet goals for product enhancement, cost reduction or quality improvement because they didn't gather this data, even when it would have been easy and inexpensive to get. The next product will be just as hard to get out the door.

In all of these areas, long, slow learning cycles increase time and cost, while they decrease quality and customer satisfaction. They lengthen the distance between you and your new product. The cumulative effects from all these barriers can kill an idea before it ever reaches a customer's hands, even if it's the best idea you have ever had.

You can choose to develop your product this way and just plan to spend lots of time dealing with the consequences. Or you can break up these long learning cycles to accelerate them.

Break Apart the Learning Cycles to Get Your Product to Market Faster

When route finding, we go a short distance, notice where we are and plan the next short distance. We look for paths of least resistance to our destination, one section at a time. We take just a little time scouting out the terrain ahead of us, to find the mountain passes, the river crossings and any trails that might already have been cleared to get us at least part of the way. We check in frequently to make sure we're on the right track, that we're still scouting ahead for obstacles and always looking for opportunities to take a shorter route to our destination.

Rapid Learning Cycles are a synchronized set of experiments to remove uncertainty before key decisions need to be made in a product development program. One Rapid Learning Cycle is two to eight weeks of focused work to help the team make better decisions when uncertainty is high and so is the impact of the wrong decision. It's a series of scouting trips to plot the shortest distance between you and your new product.

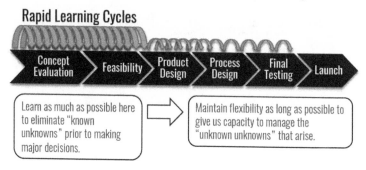

Figure 1.3: Rapid Learning Cycles

The key word is "rapid." I know that startup teams and innovation groups operate with severe shortages of money and time. This is not the time to do in-depth market studies and extensive technical investigations to make sure that every "i" is dotted before going to first release. In fact, in some circumstances, your best Rapid Learning Cycles will be built around limited releases to paying customers, so that you can evaluate their responses before finalizing decisions. Even on very long projects, such as new drugs or defense systems, you still need short learning cycles—twelve weeks is an absolute maximum.

Rapid Learning Cycles Pull Learning Earlier and Push Decisions Later

Rapid Learning Cycles work because they pull learning earlier and push decisions later. Teams delay making major commitments until they have the knowledge to make those commitments with confidence.

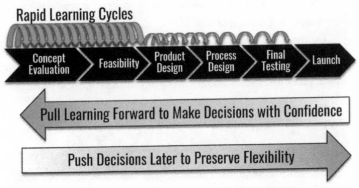

Figure 1.4: Pull Learning Forward—Push Decisions Later

Rather than write up detailed specs in Phase 1 of the PDP, the team lets key requirements float until they understand what they can deliver. Instead of pursuing one idea at a time for a tricky technical problem, the team investigates several possible answers at once. Rapid Learning Cycles provide a framework for determining the right time to make decisions, and the learning needed to make them.

Product development teams make thousands of decisions in the context of a development program. It would take an infinite amount of time to learn everything perfectly in order to make every decision absolutely correctly the first time. This is not the goal of Rapid Learning Cycles.

The goal of Rapid Learning Cycles is to focus the team's early attention on the major decisions that they must get right if they want to release a great product. Then the framework helps them structure the knowledge-building work they need to do in order to make the best decisions they can. They spend a little more time learning in order to spend less time spinning in Build–Test–Fix to repair all the fallout from decisions made too early.

When I asked the team of managers that I mentioned earlier to draw a Future State of product development, they didn't draw a straight path. But they did show an "advance team" of learners who were scouting for the best places to cross the rivers, navigating around blind canyons and digging tunnels under cliffs so that teams didn't have to go over them. The advance team scouted the terrain and mapped the path of least resistance. The rest could hit the ground running. The managers represented the team's forward motion with scribbled circles—Rapid Learning Cycles.

How Rapid Learning Cycles Get Your Best Ideas to Market Faster

Rapid Learning Cycles get your best ideas to market faster by eliminating many of those long, slow learning cycles. When you have eliminated the worst of them, these are the benefits you'll see.

Set Aggressive Dates—and Hit Them

Many product development groups and most startups deliver products to the market later than they predict—sometimes very late. This wreaks havoc in the downstream organizations, such as Operations, Supply Chain, Marketing and Sales. They struggle to launch a product that may have already missed its window of opportunity. Even if the product is still competitive, these groups see all the opportunities missed: trade shows where the product couldn't be shown, major customers that went with a competitor's product, a competitor's inferior product becoming established as the standard while the team's product languishes in prerelease mode.

Projects are usually late because the teams planned—or were told to plan—for everything to go as expected, and then the unexpected happened. Unanticipated problems trigger a lot of work that the team did not plan to do. The team may need to change decisions that are fully embedded in the product design and difficult to undo. Under the best circumstances, the amount of work added goes up dramatically as the product approaches completion, and yet this is exactly when these unexpected things tend to happen.

Traditional mitigation strategies for late design changes make things worse. Tight change control adds overhead that makes it difficult to move quickly when the team finds a problem. Locking down requirements early increases the likelihood that they will change. Design "freezes" operate the same way: forcing decisions to freeze early increases the chance that a given decision will be wrong. Forcing development teams to set aggressive dates too early drives them to take shortcuts that will hurt them later.

A product development group should be able to deliver its products on time—if the group does not set the final launch date until midway through the development process. At that point, the team members should know enough about what they understand and what they still need to learn in order to deliver a finished product that is good enough for the market it's going into. They should be able to establish a launch date that they can stick to. The more you can push decisions later, the more predictable your launch dates will be.

Rapid Learning Cycles increase teams' ability to deliver on time by directly attacking the root causes of late-breaking issues: the lack of learning up front before decisions need to be made, and the pressure to make decisions before the team is prepared to make them. By accelerating the learning process, teams get to correct errors before they become major issues, and the decisions they make are more likely to hold up under the pressure of integration in late development. By the time a team has learned enough to make the most important decisions and understand the risks they take for the things they have not yet learned, they are prepared to set an aggressive launch date—and hit it.

Fail Faster to Move On Faster

Some ideas have momentum, even when they're not good ones. Once a startup has its first round of funding or a development team has been assigned, the product takes on a life of its own. Any idea requires some things to be done that will be easy to do and some things that will be hard to do. If the idea is not going to work, the problem probably lies with the things that are hard to do. But since we are human, we tend to do the easy things first and then see all that effort wasted when a hard problem comes to the surface that requires a major redirection.

In an established company, Gate Review meetings are supposed to weed out the products that are likely to fail, before they are approved to go on to the next phase. At these meetings, a team of managers reviews the team's progress and the current state of the business case. In practice, few products get killed at these meetings. Even products with major problems get the waivers they need to continue to the next phase.

Rapid Learning Cycles help you get your best ideas to market faster by eliminating your weak ideas sooner, so that you don't waste time with them. If your idea—or your company—is completely new to the world, early Rapid Learning Cycles will focus on viability tests that can be done before you commit to anything that would be expensive to redo. This is especially important if your product is based in the real world, as opposed to the virtual world of software and Internet applications. A physical product requires investment in things that are expensive to change if you need to pivot after they are done.

Bring the Vision and Execution Closer Together

Great ideas fail in execution, and there is nothing more disappointing to an innovator than a great idea that was so poorly built that it never stood a chance. We want the final product to exceed all the promises we make to ourselves, our families, our investors and our customers.

Established companies have brand promises they need to protect, and sometimes they incorporate tools such as Failure Modes and Effects Analysis to try to eliminate quality problems within the design. But these efforts usually come too late, when the decisions embedded in the design are difficult to change. Products that don't meet quality standards in an established company tend to get stuck in Build–Test–Fix loops until they reach an acceptable quality level, which can be months or years after the product needed to be on the market to be competitive.

Rapid Learning Cycles bring execution barriers to the surface, where teams can tackle them head on. A team is not forced to commit to a fixed idea about what the product is and what quality level it needs to have until the team is ready to make commitments. If an insurmountable execution barrier leads to the need to pivot, there is a lot less momentum to overcome.

Build a Great Product You Can Afford to Make

A late product is often a compromised product that costs more for production, sales and support until the company discontinues it. It may be difficult to make, with tolerances that have to be too tight for the manufacturing process. It may require more manual assembly because it's too complex for automated manufacturing methods. It could have reliability problems that trigger extra field service calls. It could be a tough sell because the customer is hearing bad things about others' experiences with it, and sales reps may waste a lot of time on the phone with dissatisfied customers that they could have used to find new ones.

When a product is already late, or just a few weeks from launch, teams naturally focus on finding the fastest solution instead of the least expensive one. They may be given permission to make compromises that would have been unacceptable just a few weeks before. Often there isn't time to adequately test the solutions to ensure that they fix the problem before they get incorporated into the product. These late fixes can trigger new issues of their own.

Established companies deal with this problem by adding additional reviews and sign-offs to the process—but always too late to make a difference in the final product without a lot of redesign work. Instead, these mitigations generate a lot of extra work just when the team doesn't have any time to spare. Sometimes groups try to isolate new product development teams from "current product engineering" to lower costs and fix quality problems once the product is launched. This just disconnects the new product developers from the feedback they need to make the next product better, and eliminates any incentive for them to try.

Rapid Learning Cycles prevent these cost issues from occurring in the first place. The team is focused on learning the most effective way to build the product. The structure provides natural points for feedback from production partners, suppliers and support reps so that the team can take advantage of their knowledge to build a better, lower-cost product from the beginning.

Set Yourself Up for a Fast Version 2.0

Once you have the first product out, it stands to reason that the next product will be a lot easier. But sometimes teams find that they've put everything they know into the latest new product, and they have no idea where to go for Version 2.0. Sometimes Version 1.0 is so compromised that the next version will have be rebuilt from the ground up.

This is especially true if you work in an established company that has traditionally had long product development timelines. If it's going to be three years before the next product comes out, every good idea has to get into this product—or wait another three years.

But every good idea adds complexity to the product and increases the likelihood that something will go wrong somewhere, especially if the team adds them without taking the time to learn about them first.

Startups are often focused on getting their first product out the door, and their teams are exhausted when it finally ships. If they have focused on delivering the best solution, instead of an MVP, it may not be obvious to them how to evolve the product. They may not even have allowed themselves to think that far ahead.

When you are first trying to turn a great idea into a finished product, you naturally want to focus on what you need to do—and only what you need to do—to make your vision a reality.

Everything else seems superfluous, a waste of time and money. Yet that leads the team down a narrow alley without a lot of room to maneuver if something goes wrong. Over time that erodes an organization's confidence in its ability to deliver growth through innovation.

Rapid Learning Cycles encourage test-to-learn vs. test-to-ship. A little bit of experimentation in the early phases of the project can help the team preserve more flexibility later on.

It also has the benefit of giving the team a lot of places to go with the next version of the product. The team may add a technology that was promising but not quite ready, or use a material that was too expensive for an MVP, but would be interesting in a premium version of the product, or build a feature that needs a fresh user interface if it's going to work smoothly.

Team members will not only be excited to get their first product shipped, but eager to come back to work on Monday and get started on the next version. They will grow in their ability to deliver innovative solutions and then build on those to create product families and even new lines of business. They will have greater confidence in their ability to turn ideas into products and that confidence will spill over into the rest of the business.

Rapid Learning Cycles Build Confidence in Product Development's Ability to Innovate

When product developers have a history of missed timelines, quality problems, high costs and disappointing features and/or performance, their business partners lose confidence in them. The partners, and sometimes the product developers themselves, stop believing in the company's ability to innovate. They take a wait-and-see attitude about anything new that emerges from R&D, and they tell key customers to wait to purchase a new product "until they get the bugs worked out."

Long, Slow Learning Cycles Erode Confidence

When product development is one long, slow learning cycle, business partners see disappointing products that require a lot of firefighting in late development. These fires burn all of the downstream functions. Production can't meet its production plans. Supply Chain has to deal with change orders and failure to meet commitments to vendors. Marketing can't launch products effectively, and sales teams don't get the product information they need in time to meet their sales goals. It's no wonder that other functions begin to lose faith in R&D's ability to deliver, and they build plans that assume that R&D will be late.

Your brand equity and your customers' expectations can be seen as barriers to innovation, since the need to serve existing customers tends to kill immature technology rather than incubate it. Your partners may look jealously on the freewheeling environment that allows startups to try one new thing after another until they get it right.

Lack of Confidence Leads to Extreme Measures

We know that our business partners lack confidence in product development when they refuse to stake their own success on our ability to get the product out the door. Instead, there is a lot of finger-pointing between R&D's leaders and other functional leaders. This is sometimes so bad that business teams succumb to the siren song of outsourced product development or "open innovation"—both models built on the assumption that outsiders can deliver better products than the company's own engineers.

Other traditional solutions include holding R&D accountable with performance bonuses for on-time delivery, locking down requirements early and refusing to allow changes, and sometimes firing people who have led failed projects. But performance bonuses (or the lack of them) and firings simply create a climate of fear that impedes innovation as everyone plays it safe. Locking down requirements early just increases the likelihood of delivering a product that no one wants to buy.

Some experts recommend separating innovation teams from the rest of the company to keep the established organization from squashing compelling yet immature investments—so-called "skunkworks" teams. These measures keep middle managers from canceling the projects too quickly.

Other experts advocate for focusing the engineering teams on improving existing products and looking to the outside for more innovative products: design firms, outsourced engineering staff and strategic acquisitions to purchase new technologies the company can't seem to develop internally. These strategies have their place in some situations. But only a small number of truly breakthrough products have followed this path—not nearly enough to justify the disruptions they cause.

Products produced using this disconnected process are not more likely to get to market, because instead of being accelerated, learning slows down. The innovations suffer from lack of acceptance when they are ready for commercialization. The products don't integrate well into the rest of the company and can't leverage the company's core functions. If they don't get spun off, they die a slow death.

More typically, a compelling innovation collapses under the weight of all the work required to ensure that the product meets company standards once the product idea encounters the organization's internal systems, and never sees the light of day. Fortunately, there's a better way.

Raid Learning Cycles Build the Capacity for Innovation

We've found that Rapid Learning Cycles help avoid a lot of the problems that established companies have when they try to innovate. They help the innovation teams mature a technology until it's ready to release with the company's reputation behind it. They provide structured timeframes that prevent innovators from getting thrown off-course by shifting priorities and the needs of the current business. They help teams leverage the relevant aspects of the organization's knowledge base without being limited by it.

The emphasis on early learning encourages broad exploration that supports teams as they develop creative solutions to customer problems. Whether you seek growth by finding new customers for your technology or by finding new solutions for your existing customer base, your teams will be able to identify the knowledge they can leverage and the knowledge they need to build.

When your Innovation Process combines structure, agility, the ability to learn fast and the ability to know what to learn, you have an engine to drive the most disruptive innovation over all the hurdles that the status quo puts in your way.

Better Engagement and Results Rebuilds Confidence

The first step to restored confidence is engagement. Rapid Learning Cycles increase the organization's confidence in R&D by engaging partners early and often in cross-functional learning events that make the team's progress visible. The framework provides a structure for getting critical input from these downstream partners at the point in development where it will be the most useful. It builds a sense of shared responsibility for the product's success that defuses all the finger-pointing, as the functional group representatives become part of a team committed to delivering a great product.

The true benefits come when your teams experience success on a regular basis and so do your business partners. When teams uncover obstacles early in a program, they can remove them before they become sources of conflict. Partners get fewer nasty surprises at the end. The products themselves benefit from the ability to discern what knowledge can be reused, what needs to be extended and what needs to be created.

As the teams and R&D management gain more confidence, they become more tolerant of risk and more willing to explore ideas that are outside their comfort zones. They know they have the skills to evaluate ideas to find the good ones, and they know they can build the knowledge they need to reduce the risks of a good idea that may have been outside their comfort zone.

It will be easier for them to explore fields of inquiry that will lead to breakthrough innovations, because they will know that they have what it takes to understand an idea before they commit the organization's resources to the expensive work of commercializing it.

Pull Learning Forward and Push Decisions Later

If you take away just one thing from this book, let it be this: the more you can pull learning forward and push decisions later, the faster your ideas will get to the market.

This is not easy, whether you are working by yourself in a garage or as part of a team inside one of the world's largest companies. All of our natural instincts as innovators and entrepreneurs tell us to get moving.

Our hands burn with the desire to build stuff that will bring our visions to life. These are good instincts. They motivate us to go into the garage or the office every day, to bring our ideas to life and get them into the hands of customers who will appreciate them.

These instincts just need a little redirection. Before diving into your first build, take some time to review the ground between you and your vision. Ask yourself what you already know and what you need to learn to deliver the product you've promised yourself to deliver.

Then build those tunnels and bridges by focusing on what you don't know first, because those are the things that slow you down and make the easy things a lot harder than they need to be.

Instead of building the perfect system, identify the smallest piece you can build in order to learn something you need to know. Instead of delivering the perfect product that provides a full solution, deliver one piece that fulfills a specific customer need.

Use the tools we have for rapid prototyping in the virtual and physical worlds to conduct experiments and test variations, rather than throwing together a product that will have to be rebuilt later.

It's Your Product—
The Responsibility Starts with You

Most people learn how to do product development on the job. While engineering programs teach the technical side of design, and some business schools teach courses on innovation or entrepreneurship, almost everyone learns how to develop products by doing it, sometimes alongside more experienced engineers and sometimes with peers.

This is why established companies go so readily to solutions that lengthen the distance from idea to market. By pulling decisions earlier and increasing management oversight, they get the illusion of control. By exhorting people to go faster, rewarding heroic efforts and excessive overtime, and setting aggressive dates early in a project, they encourage people to take shortcuts on knowledge building that will trigger loopbacks later. Startups are more likely to throw out the rule book, but the effects are the same, and come with a higher personal cost to the innovators.

If Rapid Learning Cycles were easy and intuitive, we would all use them. Instead, they ask you to do some things that are uncomfortable:

- Invest more time and money in the "fuzzy front end" and knowledge-building experiments, to save time and money at the end.
- Delay decisions about things like final specifications, customer requirements and technical solutions in order to ensure that these decisions get made right the first time.
- Pursue multiple alternatives when you'd prefer to explore only the idea that looks the best on the surface.

If you want to get your ideas to market eventually, you can always do things the way people have always done them. No one will get fired in a Fortune 500 company for using the standard PDP, as long as things don't get too far out of hand. And most startups are supposed to fail anyway.

If you can get comfortable with the changes required by the Rapid Learning Cycles framework, however, you are well on your way to building a product development organization that can deliver products to the market faster, with fewer resources, at lower cost and with better quality. You can see your visions come to life and be even better than you imagined them.

When teams pull learning forward and push decisions later, they make better decisions that help them go straight from San Francisco to Los Angeles without a detour to New York.

CHAPTER TWO

What's Different About Rapid Learning Cycles?

I n the last chapter, I defined Rapid Learning Cycles as *a synchro-nized set of experiments to remove uncertainty before key decisions need to be made within a product development program.*

In this chapter, I'll go over that definition in much more detail and sketch out what it looks like when a product development team uses Rapid Learning Cycles to structure its work.

What's Different About Rapid Learning Cycles?

Rapid Learning Cycles take the best elements of Agile Software Development, systematic experimentation, risk reduction and knowledge capitalization to build a new approach to product development.

Agile Software Development is not enough, because Agile methods assume that the underlying technologies are well understood and that design changes can be applied immediately. For most people working with new applications of information technology (websites, apps), that's generally true. Even some types of real-world goods lend themselves to this way of working. But this book is aimed at programs that are using new technologies, new business models or new ways to reach customers. They have a lot more uncertainty than Agile Development alone can handle.

These differences become more apparent when we drill into the details of the definition of Rapid Learning Cycles.

Synchronization

Rapid Learning Cycles are synchronized across all the engineering disciplines and functional groups working on the product development program. The length of a single learning cycle is the project heartbeat, which is held constant throughout early product development.

As subteams and individuals align their work to this structure, they find that coordinating across subteams is much easier. The cadence is slow enough to allow for well-designed experiments. It's fast enough to create a sense of urgency that's often missing in advanced research or the "fuzzy front end" when a product launch may be months or years away.

Teams decide how long their learning cycles will be. They can choose to run learning cycles that take from two weeks to twelve weeks, depending upon the time it takes for the learning activities they need to close their Knowledge Gaps most of the time.

For products with a lot of mechanical engineering, the sweet spot is four to six weeks. Software and service development learning cycles can run faster—two weeks works well. Biological and pharma products require longer cycles—eight to twelve weeks.

Figure 2.1 shows that it's OK for some types of experiments, such as animal models, to extend across more than one learning cycle. It's also OK for some subteams, such as Software, to run a "double-time" cycle that is twice as fast as the rest of the group. Even with these exceptions, the team learning cycle sets the tempo for every subteam.

At the end of a learning cycle, the team comes together to share what they've learned and decide what they will do next. No subteam has had the chance to get so far out in front of the others that it needs a major course correction to get back into alignment. No one has time to do a lot of work that will be thrown away immediately because it conflicts with someone else's work.

Rapid Learning Cycles

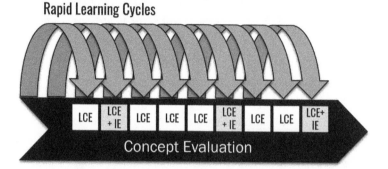

Figure 2.1: Regular Cadence of Events Synchronize the Team

Systematic Experimentation

Rapid Learning Cycles consist of a series of learning activities organized into Design–Experiment–Capture cycles. Unlike Build–Test–Fix (or the *Lean Startup* variant, Build–Measure–Learn), some of these experiments will aim to prove or disprove hypotheses the team has about markets, customers, technologies, supplier capabilities or manufacturing processes, without building the product itself. These pure experiments eliminate long, slow learning cycles by helping teams make good decisions without the time and expense of a product build.

Innovation tends to attract people with an experimental mindset, but few have had much training in the systematic methods that will make their experimentation more useful to the product teams and more valuable to the company. Instead, most engineers got accustomed to Build–Test–Fix in their university studies, as they worked problems for their engineering classes or experimented with their own ideas as students. Then the corporate world never asked them to think about what they needed to learn before they started building something.

Build–Test–Fix is not sufficient. You don't want to waste a lot of time building up a feature when a simpler test can tell you that the feature is not valued by the customer at all. Eric Ries's Build–Measure–Learn is a little better—at least the last two steps imply that the team has explicit measures for assessing performance that it will use to decide where to go in the next cycle. But it's still important to make sure that you understand what you already know—and therefore what you need to know next—and let that drive the design of your experiment.

Scientists fare a little better if they had good research experience in school, but many industrial scientists are discouraged by their peers from using the methods they learned in academia to design good experiments. They're perceived to be too slow, too analytical or too heavyweight to guide corporate R&D.

It's true that the standard of proof in a corporate R&D lab is less stringent than it is for a paper to be published in an academic journal. But when scientists try to speed up, they tend to throw out the most valuable part of their research methodology because the university standard takes so long: writing good reports that describe what they've learned to others.

As a result, the things the team's scientists and engineers learn are not broadly understood by the rest of the team and not captured for use by future teams. Engineers can't retrace the path they took to document the lessons they've learned from Build–Test–Fix. Scientists may produce reports that are too lengthy and detailed for easy consumption—but they are usually never written at all, since they take so long to produce.

To map out the shortest distance, you need to know exactly what you're building and why. What are your hypotheses? You want to make sure that you are building knowledge you can't get elsewhere—that you are not just reinventing things that others in your company already know how to do.

The hypothesis and the available knowledge determine what you need to build, how you will test it and how you will interpret the results. You may need a virtual model, a physical model, a prototype, a beta version or even a whole product in order to run a meaningful test. In every case, you want to do the minimum amount of work required to validate your hypotheses.

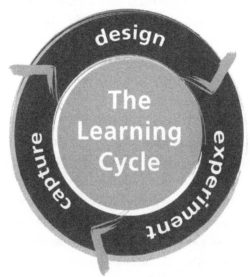

Figure 2.2: Learning Cycles of Design–Experiment–Capture

Finally, you want to write down what you've learned, in a format that allows this new knowledge to be used easily by decision makers, and re-used later by other product development teams. The reports need to be short and focused, with links to details for the people who need them.

In this book, we'll use Design–Experiment–Capture to describe the process of building and capturing knowledge to support good decision making in product development. We'll review it in detail in Chapter Eight. This method is tailored for structuring the work to be done to close Knowledge Gaps within Rapid Learning Cycles. But if your company already has a rigorous problem-solving method that's widely adopted and working well, you can use that instead.

Removing Uncertainty

Rapid Learning Cycle teams share a common mantra: "Learn before you need to decide." Before the teams make a Key Decision or adopt a concept, they determine what they need to know in order to make a good decision or adopt the right concept. Then they undertake the experiments they need to build that knowledge and confidence in the concept before committing anything.

Normally, we like to eliminate uncertainty early: it helps us feel that we're making progress toward our vision. The Rapid Learning Cycles framework treats uncertainty differently: we have it because we are missing the knowledge we need to make decisions with confidence that the decisions will lead to a great product. Making a decision without the knowledge to make a confident decision only feels like closure.

Instead, we learn to get comfortable with uncertainty so that we don't remove it too quickly. We don't shoo unanswered questions out the door prematurely to make ourselves feel better. Instead, we get the knowledge we need so that the questions won't come back again after the decision gets made.

Our goal is not to eliminate all uncertainty forever. This is product development, and there are some things we simply cannot learn until our manufacturing partners build production volumes and paying customers open their wallets. Our goal is to make sure that's all we need to learn. Everything we could learn easily, quickly and cheaply has already been learned before we have to spend serious money and time to close the uncertainty that remains.

Confident Key Decisions

Schedule pressure and overloaded resources often force product development teams to make decisions before they have enough relevant information. Even the best engineer, if forced to guess, is likely to make a choice that is suboptimal, if not wrong. These decisions get built into the product, and when they don't work out, they trigger a lot of redesign loops late in the project.

With Rapid Learning Cycles, teams take just a little time—about two hours—to identify the high-impact, high-unknown Key Decisions that are driving the project. These are the decisions that tend to cause major rework loops. The team establishes the dates by which the Key Decisions must be made so that the project is not delayed. Then it identifies the experiments that need to be done to generate the knowledge the team needs to make those decisions with confidence.

Since this is product development, we expect that time pressure and lack of available knowledge will sometimes lead the team to make a decision that gets revisited later. The goal is not to make every decision perfectly. The goal is to focus the team's attention on those Key Decisions that have the potential to either drive the project into the ditch or through to completion.

Within Product Development

Agile Software Development got its start in IT projects to build applications to automate business processes in areas such as banking, accounting and supply chain management. The first Internet developers naturally adopted Agile methods, because it took some trial and error to learn how to do real work on the Internet.

I have applied Rapid Learning Cycles only to product development programs where the goal is to deliver a product or service to a paying customer who is outside the company. Our user community has applied Rapid Learning Cycles to other contexts, such as strategic change initiatives. But I think it's important for you to understand the assumptions that drive my description of this method:

- **There is a user.** Someone will ultimately use the product to create value that is meaningful to them. The product could lead to a cleaner bathroom, a healthier body, a more profitable manufacturing line, more friends or more time to spend on other things. It doesn't matter if the value is tangible or intangible—the purpose of the product is to create value for a consumer that someone is willing to pay for. We sometimes need to know whether or not our vision of the product is as compelling to the customer as it is to us.

- **There is a buyer.** Someone will ultimately decide to pay for this product. Business models differ, so the buyer could be an advertising partner or sponsor instead of the consumer. The buyer could be an insurance company, a parent or a procurement agent rather than the end user. At some point, someone will make the economic decision that the product is delivering enough value that it's worth a financial investment. We sometimes need to know if we can set a price that is low enough to attract the buyer but high enough to be profitable.

- **There is a market.** There is a group of people who will buy and use the product. Members of the group share certain expectations about the level of quality and support they expect, the regulations that protect them, the growing pains they're willing to accept in a new product and the ones they won't tolerate, the benefits that will attract them, social networks where they can learn about the product and distribution channels where they can find it. We sometimes need to know if the market is large enough, how the social networks and distribution channels work, if there are any regulatory concerns in a given market and what benefits are the most attractive in this market.

- **There is a new product.** The objective of the project is to build something new to put into the market that will attract buyers and delight users. Even if the product is an incremental improvement from last year's release, it is still something that hasn't been done before.

In the Introduction, I mentioned that I define "product" broadly to mean any product or service that someone can buy. We use Rapid Learning Cycles to build a new product—a product that has never existed before. A simple customization or product line extension probably isn't new enough to justify a full-scale implementation of the Rapid Learning Cycles framework, but even they benefit from a learning cycle or two.

The key questions to ask yourself are . . .

What Do We Know? What Do We Need to Know?

If you know most of what you need to know—about the customer, market, regulatory environment and supply chain partners, as well as the technology—you may not need Rapid Learning Cycles at all, or you may choose to do some targeted learning cycles to close the gaps that you have. But if that's true, your product is probably not an innovation.

Successful innovation is directly related to the team's ability to systematically identify and eliminate the things you don't know that will come back to bite you. Innovators don't like to think about problems and risks. It's a lot more exciting to think about a future where the product is working well in the hands of a customer who loves it. That motivates us to come to work every day, much more than eliminating the last fifty critical defects.

Innovation is a lot more fun—and a lot more profitable—when you become ruthless about eliminating everything that stands in the way between you and your product vision. You can call them obstacles, problems, barriers, challenges—whatever you like. Your mission is to discover them and remove them as early as possible, when it's cheap and easy to do so.

In *The Lean Startup*, Eric Ries recommended that teams work toward a Minimum Viable Product (MVP). This is the simplest, least-featured product that someone would buy. Even the simplest MVP is a large-scale, expensive experiment that exposes your weaknesses to the world. You don't want your MVP to fail for a reason that you could have uncovered in a faster, easier way.

If you discover and eliminate problems as they arise in a series of haphazard Build–Test–Fix cycles, it will take a lot of cycles before you uncover all the problems, and your product will still be at risk for major defects that you don't find until it is out in the field. Even if the product performs well, you may not know why it works, which makes it difficult for you to evolve the product.

The Rapid Learning Cycles team is constantly asking itself, "What do we know, and what do we need to know?" By asking that question, they manage the "known unknowns" and scan the landscape for "unknown unknowns." When we have to make a decision based upon incomplete knowledge, at least we know that's what we have done. We know the assumptions we were forced to make and where our decisions rest on "best guesses" instead of clear facts. We have a system in place to track these guesses, so they are much less likely to be forgotten. We know what risks we take into the Execution Phase.

What Is the Fastest Way to Learn?

Finding the shortest distance between you and a finished product is all about finding the fastest way to learn.

I once worked with an organization that sent its prototype builds offshore to save money. It may be possible to get good prototypes this way, but not for this company. It took a minimum of six weeks for the prototypes to be built and sent through testing under the new process, compared to three weeks for a prototype build before this decision.

The engineers could not observe the prototype builds, and so they were unable to learn nearly as much about the manufacturability of their designs. That led to unexpected increases in defect rates and labor costs. To make matters worse, the specifications for the next prototype build were due before the test results came back from the last prototype build.

This decision caused them to go from three-week learning cycles to twelve-week learning cycles, and the products that went through this process burned up every penny of savings in prototype costs with higher support and warranty costs—and then some.

If your first product idea won't work, you shouldn't waste a moment more than it takes for you to find that out. If an engineer has made a mistake, it shouldn't take twelve weeks for that engineer to get that feedback. We want our learning cycles to turn as fast as possible.

Understand Your Core Hypothesis

Every product idea has a hypothesis at the center that encapsulates your vision for the product. For example:

> TimeYourWords! is a new electronic timer designed for writers to help them track the time they spend on their writing projects without a distracting smartphone, so that we can leverage our specialty timer expertise into a new market.

The Core Hypothesis has three dimensions:

- Customer: What customer value does the product deliver, and how does the customer interact with the product to realize that value?
  - Writers will buy TimeYourWords! because it is designed for them to track their time without being distracted, as a timer app on a smartphone might.
- Technology: What core technologies will be used to deliver the value?
  - Our known technology in delivering timers with features tailored for specialty markets.
- Business: What is the business model? How will you turn this into a profitable business?
  - Capitalizes on an opportunity in a new market.

The faster you can confirm the Core Hypothesis, the faster you can get your new product into customers' hands.

Plan Regular Go/No-Go Events

Artists, writers and composers learn early that you have to be willing to kill your creations, to take what you've learned and move on. Innovation is no different. Some product ideas won't work. Others are too early, too expensive or too difficult to implement. Organizations of any size need to be able to stop working when it's apparent that an idea has failed.

It's hard to kill something that you've nurtured, whether it is a task assigned to you by your boss or something you've been tinkering with in the garage. It's especially difficult if you've managed to convince others—family, investors, senior leaders—to buy into the dream. If you learn that it's not working, what do you do?

In a large organization, the best answer is usually to close the project and free up the people to investigate other promising ideas. Most organizations already have more promising ideas than they can investigate. It's best to cut the company's losses and give the product developers the opportunity to work on something that is more likely to succeed. That will give better results than trying to make a flawed idea work better.

If you are an entrepreneur with investors, you may need to find a way to transform your main idea into something that is more likely to work. Ideally, you used Rapid Learning Cycles to validate at least part of your Core Hypothesis before you asked for other people's money. That gives you somewhere to go if some other part of your Core Hypothesis is disproven. You can tune your technology to do something else, reach out to a different type of customer or try a different business model to earn revenue.

Since it is so hard for us to see when our own ideas don't work, you need to have an explicit time and place to do it: regular check-ins with stakeholders, advisors and mentors who can keep you honest. You also need to decide—in advance—how you will know that your idea is not working. This decision will probably be grounded in the part of the Core Hypothesis that you understand the least.

Rapid Learning Cycles provide a natural structure for these go/no-go events: they occur at the end of a learning cycle. For a rapid concept evaluation, every Learning Cycle Event may consider this question. The program sponsors or investors may choose to look at it once a quarter at an Integration Event. It probably shouldn't go much longer than that.

Learn Fast, Learn Cheap

Whenever you have a question to answer, the next step should be to ask yourself, "What is the fastest, cheapest way to learn this?" If you are used to working in an environment where everything requires a full-scale system prototype for testing, answering this question will require some creative thinking and pushback. At every point, ask yourself, "How can I validate my hypothesis with the least amount of time, effort and money?"

It greatly helps to understand the question you need to answer, and what you already know about it. That will help you design an experiment that will give you the knowledge you need with the smallest investment of time and money.

Experiment on Your Customers

Google popularized the idea that you can experiment on your own customers. This is much easier to do with an Internet product or an app than it is with a physical widget. But even in the physical world, there are ways to use your existing customer base to help you understand your product. The MVP is a large-scale customer experiment. You can also use product variants to do split testing with live customers. Rapid prototyping and mass customization techniques make this possible even in the physical world.

There are lots of ways to model a product with real customers without doing a full production run. You can send a beta version to a few hand-picked lead users. You can release a product that's difficult to set up, and provide technicians to help customers get over the rough spots. You can sell an expensive or small-run product at a loss rather than invest in large-volume production of something a customer has never seen. You can send out test versions as a bonus to a small group of customers to get their reactions.

Rapid Learning Cycles Attack Uncertainty with Knowledge

Some of the early proponents of Rapid Learning Cycles tried to claim that "You cannot move into the Execution Phase until there is no risk."

Unless you have a customer with a signed purchase order (PO) for your product, however, there is always some risk. In fact, even if you are building a product for the customer that has given you the PO, you still don't know if the customer will like the product enough to buy it again, if you will be able to sell it to someone else or if you will be able to build it.

Since all product development programs involve risk, the ability to manage that risk is what distinguishes an effective product development organization from one that struggles to get products out the door. Some organizations are so risk-averse that perfectionism and analysis paralysis infects the teams. Others are so comfortable with risk that their products get hung up in late development again and again, frustrating everyone but especially the ones who urged risk-taking to move fast.

Rapid Learning Cycles start from the premise that your customers need your best ideas in their hands. Even if it were possible for you to delay execution until you had zero risk, doing so is not the best choice for your customers.

As long as the product meets their threshold standards for quality and performance—which may be quite low if this is a product aimed at early adopters—you are better off getting it to them as quickly as possible so that both you and your customers can begin learning about the product and how it works in the real world.

At the same time, it's much easier to meet the threshold standards for quality and performance if the team makes good data-driven decisions at the right time—not too early and not too late.

Inadequate Knowledge Is the Biggest Obstacle

Rapid Learning Cycles eliminate the risk of inadequate knowledge by pulling learning forward and pushing decisions later. Teams think through what decisions need to be made—and when they need to make them. They then seek to delay these decisions as long as possible to give the team and the decision maker more time to learn.

Teams do only what they need to do to build the knowledge needed to make a decision. You can build test harnesses and subsystem prototypes rather than wait for a full prototype to test. Wherever possible, we work with models—both virtual models and physical models—to delay the moment when we commit to a choice that may have to be revisited if it's wrong.

Then we build that flexibility into the product so that we have the ability to incorporate all the knowledge we gain from real customers into the next version of our product. We don't want to learn that our Minimum Viable Product is the only product we can build.

We prioritize our work around the decisions that will cause the most problems if they have to be changed later. That's where the risk lies—and also the areas of greatest opportunity for innovation.

Build, Capture and Share Knowledge to Make Good Decisions

The purpose of a Rapid Learning Cycle is to learn, so that decision makers can make better decisions. Rapid Learning Cycles include an explicit step for capturing and sharing knowledge, to ensure that the entire organization can learn from the team's experience and to increase the likelihood that the decision maker will use this knowledge to make a decision.

In a typical product development program, teams don't believe they have time or the need to develop knowledge that can be used later. As a result, every product development team has only the team's direct experiences to learn from, and startups have a lot of growing pains when critical knowledge takes a long time to get transferred to new team members. If a group in another region or another division has learned something useful, chances are that the team will find out about it only by chance.

Rapid Learning Cycles look beyond the current product horizon to develop generalized knowledge about customers and markets, materials and design trade-offs, supplier capabilities and manufacturing processes. The knowledge they build gets captured and shared in this generalized form so that future teams and new team members can learn from it and build from it. The knowledge about the stuff that didn't work is especially valuable, both because the product design itself does not capture it and because it keeps future teams from exploring known blind alleys.

The Shift from Doing to Learning

To unlock the potential of Rapid Learning Cycles to help you find the shortest distance to your new product, you have to turn the focus from doing to learning.

We are so comfortable doing stuff: writing documentation or code, building test products, and debugging the system. But I hope you understand by now that you will get your product to market a lot faster if you accelerate learning. A team that is focused on learning fast may not do as much building, testing and fixing because that is an inefficient way to learn.

Most important, we don't do anything just because it's listed on the plan. If the activity is designed to help us learn something, make a better decision or help our downstream partners produce the product, it's a good thing to do. If we won't learn anything from the test, if the document doesn't clearly convey the information we need to transfer, if the conversation does not move the relationship forward, it's not worth our time.

The one thing product developers never have enough of is time. The way to get more of it is to maintain a laser focus on the shift from doing to learning.

In the next chapter, we'll review the core elements of Rapid Learning Cycles and the events we use to keep team members learning in sync with each other.

CHAPTER THREE

The Rapid Learning Cycles Framework

The previous two chapters have focused on why the Rapid Learning Cycles framework cuts time to market for innovation. The rest of the book will describe how to run a program with Rapid Learning Cycles.

The Base Use Case: Rapid Learning Cycles in Early Product Development

We originally developed Rapid Learning Cycles for programs in early product development, and to simplify the discussion I'll focus on that use case when I describe the elements of the framework. I'll discuss other use cases and how to adjust the framework to fit them in Section Four. Here are the operating assumptions for the base use case for the Rapid Learning Cycles framework.

- **You are at the beginning.** You may have an idea, and your first task is to qualify that idea. You may already have qualified the idea, but now you have a team assigned to develop it, and that team has not yet started serious work. You may already have done some work but realized that there are a lot of unknowns and recognized that some dedicated time spent learning now will save you a lot of time later.

- **You have organized a program to develop your idea into a product.** You will work with a team of collaborators to help you. That team can be as small as a few friends or as large as an entire company. You may think of your program as a project, and chances are, you have already thought about how to use some project management tools to help you run it. I use the term "program" to disconnect it from traditional project management practices, which don't work very well in this context.

- **You are the Program Leader, and the decisions about how to manage the team are largely in your hands.** If you decide that the team will use Rapid Learning Cycles, the team will follow you, and no one will get in your way. You may be working on your own, or in an independent business unit. You may have received permission to pilot Rapid Learning Cycles as completely as possible, ignoring conflicts with your company's standard Product Development Process (PDP). I'll cover how to integrate the Rapid Learning Cycles framework with traditional phase gate PDPs in Chapter Seven.

- **You have some experience with running teams and with project management, either traditional project management or Agile project management.** You know who your major stakeholders and development partners are, and you have invited them to be full participants in your development program. You understand your budget and the overall timeframe for delivering the new product. Ideally, this is a flexible target during the early stages that the team will lock down a little later.

It is possible to start using Rapid Learning Cycles in the middle of a program, but the team will have accumulated a lot of "knowledge debt"—decisions that were made without having the knowledge to make them correctly. I'll describe how to adapt the framework to this situation in the Chapter Fourteen.

If you are working in a startup or developing a product as an entrepreneur, this framework can help you as well. If you are a Lean Startup aficionado, this book will help you learn how to execute the Lean Startup model.

A few times in this chapter, I refer to "traditional project management." Traditional project management requires project managers to put together detailed schedule and budget forecasts that leaders may use to measure project variances. It requires a lot of documentation, such as Marketing Requirements Documents, Technical Specifications, Risk Management Plans, etc. The project managers spend much of their time working with the PDP checklists, documentation and project plans, and preparing status updates for leadership teams.

Unlike traditional project management, the Rapid Learning Cycles framework is designed to be flexible and to adapt to a wide variety of programs. As you read through these descriptions and the step-by-step instructions available on the website for the key elements of the framework, remember that there are no Six Sigma process auditors walking around with clipboards, evaluating your compliance with these guidelines. Ultimately, how you go from here to your new product is entirely up to you.

The Elements of the Framework

The framework for Rapid Learning Cycles includes the Core Hypothesis, Key Decisions, Knowledge Gaps, activities, deliverables and a series of events to help you manage them. The framework elements work together to help pull knowledge out of the program when it's needed, and they help your team maintain its focus on learning instead of doing.

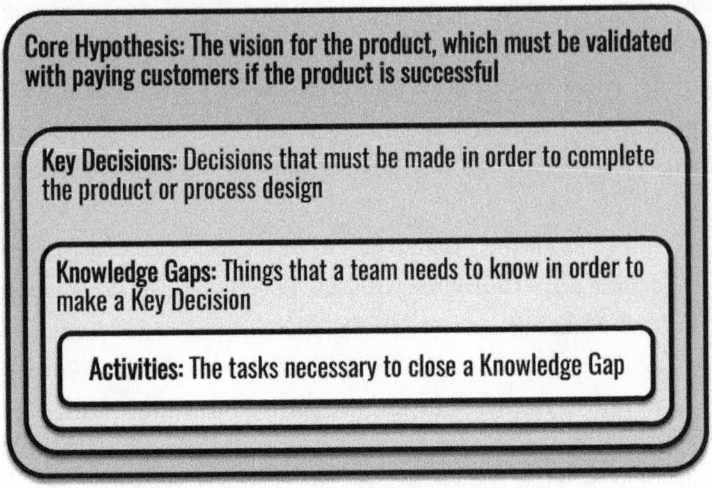

Core Hypothesis: The vision for the product, which must be validated with paying customers if the product is successful

Key Decisions: Decisions that must be made in order to complete the product or process design

Knowledge Gaps: Things that a team needs to know in order to make a Key Decision

Activities: The tasks necessary to close a Knowledge Gap

Figure 3.1: The Elements of the Rapid Learning Cycles Framework

Core Hypothesis

I described the Core Hypothesis in the last chapter as a way to accelerate learning. In the context of the Rapid Learning Cycles framework, the Core Hypothesis is a short description of the product vision that the team develops during one of their first meetings together. The team develops it together so that all team members are aligned about the product's most important objectives.

The Core Hypothesis may change as the team deepens its understanding of the technology, customers and markets. In fact, if it's a truly new idea, the Core Hypothesis often changes a lot as the team learns more about potential customers and markets. But it should not drift. When it changes, the program team and all the stakeholders need to know that it changed and why, so that they all continue working in the same direction.

The Core Hypothesis will point the team towards some of the most important early learning they can do: develop better knowledge about the concept's soundness as a product. The team will either validate the assumptions embedded in the Core Hypothesis or demonstrate that the product concept has some fundamental flaws before the company wastes much time and money on it.

Either of these outcomes is a win for the team and for the company. An early "no-go" decision spares precious R&D time for better programs.

Key Decisions

A Key Decision is a significant decision that has high impact on a product's ultimate success, and that the team does not have the knowledge to make with confidence. We handle these decisions carefully because they make or break the program.

A product development team will make thousands of decisions before the product launches. But not all of those decisions have the same importance. Some are relatively easy to change later. Others affect only a small part of the system. These low-impact decisions don't need special attention because if the team gets it wrong, either they can change it easily or it won't matter in the end. Key Decisions are the ones that the team needs to get right the first time, or the product will go on a long detour.

Other decisions leverage known solutions. Many arise naturally out of the team members' experience and the knowledge readily available to them. Some decisions get imposed on the team by technology or market constraints. Key Decisions are the ones that enable the product to do something new, unique or different than previous products.

Key Decisions have high impact on the success of the product. They often dictate the product's ability to fulfill the Core Hypothesis, with a direct relationship to customer value. They also tend to drive other decisions. For example, the choice of technology platform may dictate the markets you can sell to, the regulatory requirements you have to meet and customers' expectations for level of quality at launch.

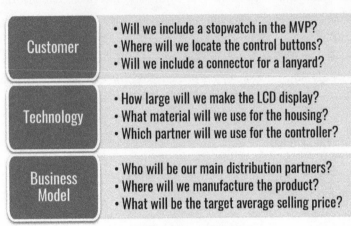

Figure 3.2: Examples of Key Decisions

Key Decisions require you to build knowledge that you don't have to-day. They have Knowledge Gaps. If you already know what you need to know to make a decision—or if the knowledge required will be developed out of other decisions, then the decision is not a Key Decision. The work of a Rapid Learning Cycles team is largely the work of closing the Knowledge Gaps that arise from Key Decisions.

Programs vary in their number of Key Decisions. Some incremental product development programs may have only one or two—or perhaps none at all. Programs to turn an idea into an innovation will often have a large number of Key Decisions.

It's important to zoom in on the Key Decisions because there is never enough time to learn everything a team would like to know. Some things are impossible to know until the product is out in the field, and other things are very costly or time-consuming to learn. The team needs to think strategically about how to maximize the value of the time they have to invest in learning. The Program Leader focuses the team's learning on the Key Decisions to help them recognize the knowledge that is most important for them to build: the most important Knowledge Gaps.

Knowledge Gaps

A Knowledge Gap is something you need to know. It may be something you need to know in order to close a Key Decision, something needed to deliver on a feature or performance gain, or something necessary to ensure that the product is safe and reliable enough. Teams always have more Knowledge Gaps than they can close. Much of the "art" of leading a Rapid Learning Cycles program is learning to prioritize: which Knowledge Gaps to close early, which ones to defer and which ones to consciously leave open.

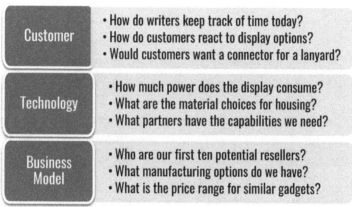

| Customer | • How do writers keep track of time today?
• How do customers react to display options?
• Would customers want a connector for a lanyard? |

| Technology | • How much power does the display consume?
• What are the material choices for housing?
• What partners have the capabilities we need? |

| Business Model | • Who are our first ten potential resellers?
• What manufacturing options do we have?
• What is the price range for similar gadgets? |

Figure 3.3: Examples of Knowledge Gaps

By definition, every Key Decision has at least one Knowledge Gap to close before the decision can be made. When the team creates the first-pass list of Knowledge Gaps, they turn to their map of Key Decisions to identify the Knowledge Gaps related to those decisions. Then the team goes further out to look for other Knowledge Gaps, some of which may take precedence over Knowledge Gaps related to Key Decisions.

Your team's first list of Knowledge Gaps will probably be long and overwhelming. The team will immediately whittle the list down to something manageable by establishing priorities. Your team can move into learning a lot faster if they work together to establish the Knowledge Gaps they will close first.

Activities

Activities are the things that end up on most project management plans: Run the X test suite. Write the POs for the components needed for Prototype B. The team does some of those things to close Knowledge Gaps, some to manage the program, and some to produce the deliverables that partners need in order to make the product. Activities are where the team spends almost all of its time, so it's no wonder that they demand a lot of the team's focus.

From a Rapid Learning Cycles perspective, the trouble with activities is that teams tend to focus on them to the exclusion of everything else. The project manager or the team puts together a plan, and then they execute the plan—even if the plan no longer makes sense. People are used to sharing their activities in meetings, and so that's what they do—instead of sharing what they learned, they share what they did.

If you've grown up in a traditional product development organization, activities represent your comfort zone. Traditional project management is all about measuring activities: planning them, updating status as activities get completed, measuring conformance to the plan. They are what you talk about at meetings, what you use to gauge performance and productivity, and what you communicate to your managers and peers to demonstrate that you are earning your keep. Even with Agile Project Management, the focus is on activities: "Write the code to execute this User Story." Or "Put together three design concepts for the Message Window."

You have to get away from this mindset to embrace Rapid Learning Cycles. In a Rapid Learning Cycles program, activities have no value in and of themselves. They have value only if they contribute to closing Knowledge Gaps, making Key Decisions or implementing those decisions. If you ever find yourself doing an activity that does not relate to Knowledge Gaps, Key Decisions or implementation, stop doing it immediately. Instead, ask yourself why you're doing it, and then redirect your time into activities that will help you learn.

We spend very little time on managing activities—as little time as possible. We do not write status reports to update others on our activities. We do not plan them more than one learning cycle in advance. We update our Activity Plan weekly, in an event that is designed to get people in and out so that they can go back to learning. We set up our other events to keep activities out of the room.

Deliverables

If a traditional product development team spends a lot of time doing activities, those activities are focused primarily on producing deliverables. The traditional PDP consists of deliverables lists that teams must produce in order to pass the gates.

We still need deliverables, although the list may need to be simplified. The deliverables are the means we have to document our decisions and share them with other teams, especially our suppliers, manufacturing partners, regulatory agencies and sales teams. But we handle them differently to reflect what they are: a bundle of decisions. Some of these are Key Decisions and others are not.

Most PDPs treat both of these types of decisions as the same, and encourage or even force teams to make Key Decisions too early. In the Rapid Learning Cycles framework, we distinguish between Key Decisions and ones that are not.

With the ones that are not Key Decisions, the goal is to minimize the amount of time it takes to capture the decision and implement it. Since the decision is either a known solution or a low-impact guess, it can be made at any time, although early is generally better.

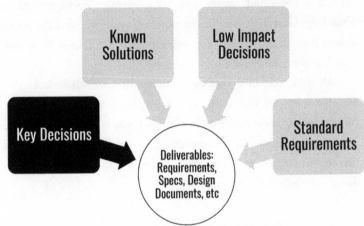

Figure 3.4: Deliverables Are Bundles of Decisions

Key Decisions need to be made at the right time, with the best available knowledge. If we push to make Key Decisions too early, then we are likely to revisit them later when it's more expensive and painful to undo them. If we guess, we are much more likely to be wrong because it's new to us.

We handle Key Decisions in deliverables with placeholders: "This decision will be made at the September 30 Integration Event." We can also put in provisional decisions: "The current plan is to use XYZ supplier's solution, and we will finalize that decision on September 30 after we receive and test samples."

Is It a Key Decision, a Knowledge Gap, an Activity or a Deliverable?

It's easy to confuse Key Decisions, Knowledge Gaps, activities and deliverables, especially at first.

A Key Decision represents a true choice: "Shall we open Door #1 or Door #2?" Sometimes, you'll learn that Door #1 has a man-eating tiger behind it. Sometimes, you'll learn that Door #2 also has a man-eating tiger. Sometimes, you'll discover that you have Doors 3, 4 and 5 to choose from. But even if you don't like the choices, you do have them, including the choice to walk away, opening none of the doors. You can cancel the program or take it in an entirely new direction.

Knowledge Gaps represent objective facts that you need to learn: "What's behind Door #1?" They have fact-based answers: "There is a man-eating tiger behind Door #1." It may not be easy to get that fact without opening the door. When you try to run experiments to find the facts, you may find that your data is inconclusive or open to interpretation. Nevertheless, the answer does exist, even if it's difficult to get.

It's especially important to avoid mixing up Key Decisions and Knowledge Gaps with activities or deliverables. "Run a simulated tracking experiment in the desert" is an activity. "How does the proposed tracking system work under conditions of high heat and low humidity?" is a Knowledge Gap. You may be able to close that Knowledge Gap without going to the desert.

"Write the specifications document" is an activity that will lead to a deliverable. "What are the marketing requirements?" is a bundle of decisions, some Key and some not. We separate out the Key Decisions and then capture the rest in the Marketing Requirements Document as an activity: "Write the first pass MRD."

Cadence

The Rapid Learning Cycles framework is, by definition, cyclic. The program is broken down into time intervals, with events that repeat for every interval of time. Every learning cycle ends with a Learning Cycle Event, where teams share the knowledge they created since the last Learning Cycle Event, and then plan the next one. Every learning cycle is the same length so that it functions as the heartbeat of the program, changing only if it's clear that the heartbeat is too fast or too slow.

It turns out that the cyclic nature of the program structure has a lot of power, because it has cadence. The regular, predictable rhythm helps the team cope with the uncertainty that swirls around them. When it seems as though everything is changing underneath the team members' feet every day, this cadence gives the team something stable to hang on to, and that makes it much easier to tolerate the uncertainty. It's easier to keep Key Decisions open, to probe for Knowledge Gaps and challenge assumptions, because the team has a steady cadence holding it together.

When a raft goes through rapids, a pilot steers the raft, but for everyone else, the objective is to keep paddling in sync with one another. Paddling provides the forward momentum that helps the raft cut through the churning water without getting diverted into obstacles by the current. Cadence works the same way on a project with high turbulence: it keeps everyone pulling in the same direction and generates forward momentum to carry the team over obstacles.

Cadence makes the team's progress a lot more visible, by putting regular markers in the road ahead that the team can use to measure its pace. Just as racers use distance markers as check-in points to ensure that they are going fast enough to hit their time goal, Rapid Learning Cycles teams use learning cycle boundaries to assess their progress toward their product vision. If a given Knowledge Gap is proving to be difficult to close, everyone is going to see that right away. If the team is making good progress, the stakeholders will see it in the results the team reports at the end of the cycles.

The Program Heartbeat

The learning cycle establishes the program's heartbeat, and it's normally two to eight weeks long. This heartbeat keeps the team members working in sync with each other. They get skilled at breaking their work down into pieces that fit within a learning cycle—especially designing experiments to close Knowledge Gaps—so that they have something meaningful to report at the end of a cycle. They learn to time their activities to the pace of the overall program. The pace normally feels a bit fast at first, but the team gets used to it, and then it pulls the program through the uncertainty.

Since everyone is on the same cycle length, it's easier for a team to coordinate the work so that team members don't accidentally collide at the interfaces or when using scarce resources such as model shops and test equipment. This eliminates a lot of the coordination that the project manager would normally need to do, because the learning cycles themselves perform the coordination function.

A learning cycle is long enough for a team to learn something meaningful, but not long enough for it to get sidetracked or diverted from the main objective. If some members of the team learn something surprising, it's not very long before the rest of the team knows it, too. If a problem comes up, it has no place to hide.

Interlocking Cadences

Activity updates happen at a faster cadence—daily, weekly or biweekly. They always line up with the cadence for learning cycles; a team with three-week learning cycles can have daily or weekly activity updates, but not biweekly.

The team times the Last Responsible Moment for Key Decisions to line up with the end of a learning cycle, and holds an Integration Event when that Key Decision will be made. Integration Events do not have to occur on a regular pattern, but it's good to hold an Integration Event at least once a quarter on most projects.

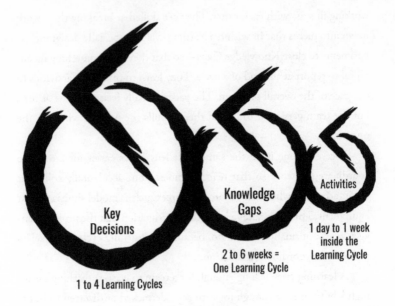

Key
Decisions

Knowledge
Gaps

Activities

1 day to 1 week
inside the
Learning Cycle

2 to 6 weeks =
One Learning Cycle

1 to 4 Learning Cycles

Figure 3.5: Interlocking Cadences

Some teams are able to move a lot faster than others. We often find that software teams work best on short cycles, while mechanical teams need longer cycles. Having different teams working at different cadences is OK as long as the cycles line up: three weeks / six weeks or two weeks / four weeks are common patterns that work well. I've run programs with one-week cycles, but that is too fast for almost everyone.

Pull Events

What happens at the end of a learning cycle? We hold an event to close the previous cycle and open the new one. These events pull knowledge through the program. Engineering and scientific work tends to expand to fill the available time—and so we place a strict limit on that time before requiring teams to share what they have learned.

Every learning cycle is a time box: a fixed amount of time that the team will use to learn as much as it can about its Knowledge Gaps. Within that time, team members can structure their work in any way that will maximize learning. If it's helpful, they can map out the activities into a short project plan, or they can work with less structure, allowing the previous day's results to dictate today's work—so long as they have something meaningful to report at the end of the cycle.

The events themselves do not move. The dates can be fixed on the calendar between now and the next major phase transition for your program. For teams used to delaying Status Updates and Gate Reviews if they need more time, this can cause a bit of culture shock at first. These events are not about looking good for managers. They are about sharing what the team has learned—including everything that didn't work, everything that's raw and unfinished, experiments that failed. You want to surface problems right away. A team that wants more time is a team that needs to talk about what's in its way.

Rapid Learning Cycles programs have three types of events that are synchronized with one another, plus one event to get off to a good start. These events keep the team on track and help them focus. They sustain the program cadence and help the team make the shift from doing to learning.

We keep these events separate, even if they occur right next to each other. Even if the meetings are separated by only a five-minute stretch break, the change of context helps the group maintain the shift from doing to learning.

Here are the four types of events that program teams will conduct within the Rapid Learning Cycles framework:

- **Project Kickoff Event.** A face-to-face Kickoff Event is essential to establish a good Rapid Learning Cycles framework for your team. The more distributed your team is around the world, the more you need this. You don't have time to waste on miscommunication and misalignment. In this event, you will align the team on the program's Core Hypothesis. You will establish the Key Decisions that drive the program. You will list and then prioritize your major Knowledge Gaps. Finally, you will put it all together into a Learning Cycles Plan that establishes the team's cadence and makes the team's work visible to everyone.

- **Status Event.** This is where the team reports on the status of its activities. The purpose of this meeting is to immediately surface problems that are getting in the way. Some teams want to hold one every day, but other teams find that once per week, or once every two weeks, is enough.

  We hold Status Events as standup meetings: people literally stand up, rather than sitting around a conference table. This keeps them short and focused on action. Every person on the team reports: "Here's what I got done. Here's what I'm going to do. Here's where I need help." The only allowed responses are, "Thank you" or "I can help with that."

  Your role as the Program Leader is to keep the meeting moving, and to shut down any efforts to solve problems during the meeting. That just wastes time for everyone who is not engaged in the specifics of the problem.

- **Learning Cycle Event.** This is the event focused on Knowledge Gaps, and the purpose of the meeting is knowledge sharing. You will hold these events on a regular cadence of every two to eight weeks.

  Learning Cycle Events are the place where teams share what they've learned over the last learning cycle: what Knowledge Gaps they have closed, which ones are proving to be difficult to close, and which new ones have turned up. Then the team members decide together what they will do in the next learning cycle and makes adjustments to their Learning Cycles Plan.

- **Integration Event.** This is the event focused on Key Decisions. The primary purpose is to make those Key Decisions with everyone who needs to participate. The team will also review the major decisions that have been made and establish the direction for the next set of learning cycles. The timing for Integration Events can be adjusted to meet the needs of the program, but should always line up with the end of a learning cycle. The Learning Cycles Plan often gets a major update at this event, and you may invite stakeholders—R&D leaders, investors and perhaps even key customers or vendors—to participate in part of the event.

Status Event
At Least Weekly
Team / Subteams

Learning Cycle Event
End of Every Learning Cycle
Team + Experts

Integration Event
Every One to Four Learning Cycles
Team + Decision Makers

Figure 3.6: Rapid Learning Cycle Events

Some teams in the earliest stages of Concept Evaluation may hold an Integration Event at the end of every cycle, where they evaluate the evidence to see if early data collection seems to validate the Core Hypothesis. They may make a continue/stop decision at every event for a while. In the middle of the program, Integration Events are held every two to four cycles. Then, at the end of the program, Integration Events line up with learning cycles again, except that the Integration Event focuses on a specific prototype build or pilot run.

- **Reflection Event.** This is the event that focuses on the health of the Rapid Learning Cycles framework. It normally takes place at the end of the first few Learning Cycle Events, and then perhaps at the Integration Event. It's an opportunity for the team to reflect, give you feedback on the framework, and decide as a team to make adjustments. If you are going to change the cadence of your learning cycle, this is where you decide to make that change. The reporting templates, agendas, meeting place, size and scale of Knowledge Gaps and Key Decisions are other items that often come up here.

  If this is your first experience with Rapid Learning Cycles, these events will help you adjust the method until it fits you well. Each Reflection Event will help you tailor the framework to fit your own environment. Even established teams need to periodically take time out to see if there is anything that can be changed so that the team works better together.

Chapter Seven covers these events in more detail. The next section describes the tools we use to manage all of these interlocking events.

Project Management Tools for Rapid Learning Cycles

Teams adopting the Rapid Learning Cycles framework for the first time often stumble over the basics of how to manage a program that has such an unconventional structure. Rapid Learning Cycles are, by definition, fast and iterative. Teams work best when they establish and maintain a regular rhythm for short-term, medium-term and long-term updates to their Learning Cycles Plan that gives them the agility they need to respond to the new knowledge they develop.

Two additional factors make things even more complicated. First, not all Knowledge Gaps can be closed in the context of a product that needs to get to market quickly. The team will need to take smart risks, make some decisions based on limited information and then watch carefully to make sure that their assumptions hold true as the program progresses. Second, the answers to some questions depend upon the answers to other questions. A team cannot always choose to close the easiest or the least expensive Knowledge Gaps first.

Project managers quickly learn that traditional project management methods break down. Gantt charts get too complex and difficult to update. Issues lists get clogged with unanswered questions. It's difficult to set a firm schedule with so many different decision trees, convergence points and alternative paths.

We also need to track several levels of dependencies. Some Key Decisions are true "showstoppers"—if we cannot close the Knowledge Gaps we need to make a good decision, or if the answer is no, the rest of the work will stop. This may drive the team to delay starting the work to close other Knowledge Gaps until it knows that the program is going to go forward past that Key Decision.

Knowledge Gaps and activities often have a natural sequence to them, with some work that needs to finish before other work can start. Gantt charts show these dependencies, and simple ones can help the team work out the sequence. But most project management software will drive a project manager to include increasing levels of detail, until the plan is incomprehensible to anyone except the person who built it and time-consuming to update as things change.

To keep track of all these moving parts, we use multilevel planning with rolling windows. Using this technique, the team does not try to track everything in one monstrous plan. Instead, only the top-level plan extends all the way to Launch. As the team drills down into more detail, the planning windows get shorter and shorter. I'll describe the typical plans and their planning windows in the next chapter.

It turns out that the best way to manage all of this complexity is with the simplest of tools.

- **Visual Management Board for the Learning Cycles Plan.** This is a physical board—or a simple virtual equivalent—with a grid. The columns are the learning cycles and Integration Events. The rows are either subteams, functional groups or individuals who will work to close Knowledge Gaps. Knowledge Gaps and Key Decisions go into this grid as "sticky notes" placed in either the learning cycle where the team will begin to close the Knowledge Gap or the Integration Event where the Key Decision will be made. The completed grid is the Learning Cycles Plan.

- **Key Decisions Log.** This log is a spreadsheet with one row for each Key Decision. The log keeps track of each Key Decision: the Last Responsible Moment to make the decision, the name of the responsible decision maker and the decision that was made. A numbering scheme makes it easy to link Key Decisions with their Knowledge Gaps.

- **Knowledge Gaps Backlog.** The backlog is another spreadsheet, usually a tab in the same workbook as the Key Decisions log. It keeps track of every Knowledge Gap: who owns it, when it was closed, and a short summary of the resolution. The template gives special attention to Knowledge Gaps that will not be closed, because they represent the program's major areas of risk.

- **Knowledge Gaps Report.** Your team members won't write lengthy documents to capture the results of their experimentation—they won't have time, and you don't need that level of detail. They also won't bore each other with long slideshows. Instead, they will write simple, one-page reports that capture the most important things that the team needs to know, so that they can share what they have learned with one another.

    This report is often in the form of an "A3 Report"—a report written on a single side of an A3 (or tabloid)-sized sheet of paper.

This report size supports communicating the right amount of information to encourage good decision making. It can also be letter sized (although it will be a bit tight for most purposes). Or it can be a single slide that's formatted to project well on screen, with at most three backup slides containing additional information.

- **Key Decisions Report.** This report looks similar to the Knowledge Gap Report, except that it describes the resolution of a Key Decision: what decision was made, who made it, the rationale for the decision and the implications for the rest of the project.
- **Team Knowledge Repository.** Depending on the size and distribution of your team, you may have an online collaboration system or a simple file share for maintaining your program's knowledge. It's less important to have the right tool than it is to make sure that the documents inside the tool are well organized and that every team member has access to it, for both uploading and downloading files.

These simple tools keep project management overhead to a minimum so that you as the Program Leader can focus on guiding your team toward effective learning to close Knowledge Gaps and make good Key Decisions. Since the team maintains the Learning Cycles Plan together, the group is well aligned on what they need to do and how to coordinate with each other. The Knowledge Gap and Key Decision Reports replace a lot of heavy documentation that doesn't get done well in a traditional program because there isn't time to write it.

The Rapid Learning Cycles website has downloadable templates for these tools, and Chapter Seven describes how to use them in the context of Learning Cycle and Integration Events.

PART TWO

The Rapid Learning Cycles Program

CHAPTER FOUR

The Foundations of the Framework

I n this chapter, I'll review some of the foundational concepts that underlie the Rapid Learning Cycles framework: Agile Development, multilevel planning, risk elimination and knowledge capitalization. These concepts work synergistically in the framework to deliver the benefits of accelerated learning and delayed decisionmaking.

Our workshop participants and clients tell us that the framework delivers results most consistently when they run their programs tightly, adhere as closely as possible to the framework as I teach it, and hold firmly to the principles described in this chapter for changes that they do make.

Agile Program Management

The Rapid Learning Cycles framework is grounded in Agile Development methods for managing programs. Agile Development was defined during the great wave of computerization, when IT groups converted paper business processes into software applications. Agile methods are optimized for working with a customer who knows the business process well, but does not know much about software.

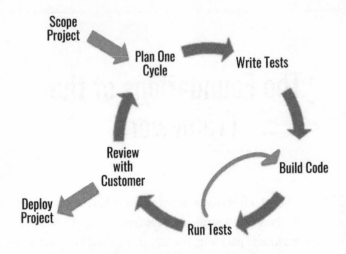

Figure 4.1: A Simplified Agile Development Process

The Agile Software Development methods arose out of the all-too-common frustration of developing a product that met all the specifications but either was unusable or the customers hated it. The software developers had not set out to write a bad application, nor had the customers intentionally misled the developers into focusing on the wrong things. The problem was that the developers didn't know the business domain, and the domain experts didn't know how software was built. All the specs in the world couldn't overcome those major knowledge gaps.

It also took a long time to build anything. System architects would design an entire system, then break it down into modules. Coders would implement those modules. Then the architects would try to put the system together. It never worked the way the design predicted that it would. Programs would get stuck at 90% complete, but that final 10% was the hardest part, and all of it was saved for the end.

Finally, knowledge work of any kind expands to fill the available time. Software development is never done early, because there are always more tests, more commenting, more code reviews that can be done. Without a firm deadline, it's hard to know when "good enough" is good enough to ship.

Agile Software Development breaks down the artificial barriers between developers and customers, eliminates the tedious rework of updating requirements documents that change constantly, surfaces integration problems early rather than waiting until the end, and provides better guidance for timing expectations.

Short, Fast Learning Cycles to Close Knowledge Gaps

In early development, developers learn faster if customers can react to something tangible. It takes pages and pages of documentation to describe the data entry screen for an invoice—and many companies did exactly that. It is much simpler for a developer to work with a customer to convert an invoice into an interface window in a series of small steps so that the developer can check and adjust before she gets too far down the wrong path. These Build–Test–Fix cycles can spin very fast in user interface design, especially if the team uses good prototyping and automated test tools.

When I was developing the estimation system in college, I didn't write specifications. I first sought to replicate the worksheets and proposal forms my boss used. Then I layered in estimation functionality for things like paint, wallboard and tile. I would add a feature, test it against existing proposals to see if it worked and validate the input and output with him along the way. With just two people working on a small, well-defined problem, we didn't need much planning or coordination. Programs with larger teams need better communication, and cadence helps keep everyone in sync.

If you are going to spin cycles of Build–Test–Fix, it helps to make them all the same length so that the teams get the benefits of cadence.

However, it's not that far from there to Rapid Learning Cycles. You just need to add some scientific rigor to the experimentation that goes on in Build–Test–Fix, and right-size the cycles to meet the needs of the functional groups that have Knowledge Gaps to close.

Minimum Documentation to Delay Decisions

In some forms of Agile, such as Extreme Programming, the team produces no documentation—or very little. Architectural models get drawn on whiteboards. Coding standards make the code "self-documenting" to replace specifications that are usually out of date. Prioritized feature lists replace detailed requirements documents. Prototypes replace user interface specifications.

The early Agile experts advocated for minimum documentation primarily because developers hate to write it and because it's always out of date. But the true benefit is that a lack of documentation drives teams to delay decisions until the code needs to be implemented.

Other forms of Agile have developed the concept of the "User Story" or "Use Case"—a narrative description of how a customer will use a feature, and how the system will respond. They are short, simple documents that can easily be adjusted by the developer and the customer-partner as they learn.

With Rapid Learning Cycles, we use short, simple documents to capture the knowledge we build. Knowledge Gap Reports and Key Decision Reports convey the most important information in the least amount of time.

Timeboxes

Writing, research, coding and engineering work all tend to expand to fill the available time. Agile Development solves this problem with timeboxes. With a timebox, a feature or a user story has an allocated amount of time that it will require to implement, and the developer is expected to deliver within this time, even if it means cutting scope on the feature to get it done within the timebox. A developer may be assigned more than one user story within a cycle; if so, he or she is expected to complete them all within the timebox.

Then the feature or story is either "done" or "not done"—there is no 50 percent done or 90 percent done. Since the developer is getting frequent feedback from the customer, he or she is empowered to negotiate with the customer about what it means to be "done." Perhaps adding that final menu option wasn't as important as moving on to the next thing.

Each Rapid Learning Cycle is a timebox, and Knowledge Gaps are either "closed" or "not closed." The team members will learn as much as they can about a Knowledge Gap in a learning cycle, report on what they have learned, and then make a recommendation. After a team has been through a few cycles, it should be rare that a team member asks for—and gets—more time.

Scrum for Rapid Learning Cycles

Scrum is the most common Agile Software Development method I encounter. It has a rigorous structure and a certification process to ensure that the method's teachers understand how the method works and encourage ScrumMasters to implement the entire system instead of just pieces of it. There are a number of books, websites, consultants and training programs to support it.

The default Scrum structure defines four-week "sprints" with daily "standup meetings" in between. The plan changes only at the Sprint Planning Session. In between these meetings, the plan is stable. Teams write up User Stories to define a piece of work that goes onto a Backlog. The Backlog is a prioritized list of all the User Stories that the team needs to complete in order to finish the system. Each User Story gets assigned a number of story points that reflect the estimated effort to deliver the story, and teams keep track of the number of story points they can deliver in one sprint.

As my clients and I developed the Rapid Learning Cycles framework, we encountered many teams who already knew Scrum, and we blended our ideas about learning cycles, Key Decisions and Knowledge Gaps with Scrum's program management method. User Stories became Knowledge Gap and Key Decision reports. Sprints merged into Learning Cycles. We adapted the visual management methods and the standup meetings but provided more options for teams working on different types of programs.

Today, a team doesn't need to know how to use Scrum to use Rapid Learning Cycles—in fact, knowing Scrum may get in the way. It's better to maintain a single vocabulary for the key elements of the system that recognizes the difference between building a product for the virtual world versus building one that must obey the laws of physics.

Multilevel Plans

In 2011, I visited Suzanne van Egmond at the Philips facility in Drachten, The Netherlands. I came to see Suzanne and her team because they had begun to use an innovative, multilayered approach to planning in product development. I described van Egmond's planning system in my first book, *The Mastery of Innovation*, and it became an important element of the Rapid Learning Cycles framework.

As the Program Leader, you need to be able to view the program at different levels. At a high level, you know when the product needs to reach the market and the major milestones along the way. You probably established that schedule yourself, and if you are a big-picture person, that may be the only planning you like to do. But that's not enough to run a program like this—there are too many side alleys and distractions that can pull the team away from the shortest path.

However, a detailed plan won't work either. You may be a methodical person who likes to plan everything to the smallest detail. If that's the case, you'll spend too much time trying to keep this plan updated in the midst of all the uncertainty, and your team will always see the plan as your plan—not their plan. Instead, we plan ahead only as far as we can see.

The Rapid Learning Cycles framework works best with four levels of plans reflecting four degrees of visibility, and three different rolling windows for keeping the plan current.

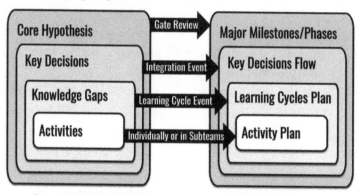

Figure 4.2: Multilevel Planning in the Rapid Learning Cycles Framework

- **Major Milestones Plan.** This is the top-level plan that spells out the path to the market. It shows the entire lifecycle of the program, from idea to launch. If you have a phase gate process, this level will show the gates, but those should not be the only milestones in the plan. Other major milestones, such as key technology or partner selections or customer reviews, need to be on this plan for you to see the path ahead. You develop this plan in collaboration with sponsors and stakeholders, and you present it to the team as a given. You will review it and update it when you hit the next major milestone, at a Kickoff Event to launch the next major phase of development.

- **Key Decisions Plan.** This plan shows the sequence of decisions that need to be made to get to the next major milestone. It may include a few Key Decisions past that milestone if that helps you to see and understand the sequence. You may also choose to extend this plan only two or three Integration Events ahead, even if the next milestone is still months away when you reach the last event. The team makes the first version of this plan in the first Kickoff Event, when they put the Key Decisions into a sequence. You can make it into a flowchart with boxes and arrows, or you may find that the list of Key Decisions is enough for this level. We review this plan at Integration Events to see if the Key Decisions still reflect program needs, and we plan out the next section of this level when we reach the next major milestone or the final Integration Event on the plan.

- **Learning Cycles Plan.** This plan identifies Knowledge Gaps to support Key Decisions. The team creates it at the Kickoff Event, and it extends to the end of the phase. Since this plan changes constantly, we use simple tools: sticky notes on a whiteboard, or a virtual equivalent. Whatever tool we use, teams update the plan themselves in real time during their events. We do major updates to this plan at Integration Events. At the end of these events, we review the plan for the Knowledge Gaps to get to the next Integration Event, and we add the Knowledge Gaps we need to get to the Integration Event that follows. We do minor updates to this plan at Learning Cycle Events.

- **Activity Plans.** The lowest level defines the team's day-to-day work: the individual steps they take to run their experiments and produce the team's deliverables. In the Rapid Learning Cycles framework, we assume that the subteams are capable of managing this level of the program on their own. As the Program Leader, you may help develop these Activity Plans, review them or have nothing to do with them as long as the team is on track. We plan activities only for the next learning cycle. There is no reason to go any further. The person or team responsible for closing Knowledge Gaps is the one that puts together this plan, and it can be a visual plan or a Gantt chart showing dependencies—whatever is most helpful. It is not created during any event with the entire team. While the activities themselves get reviewed at Status Events, the Activity Plan does not get a whole team review, in order to reinforce the shift from doing to learning.

While this might sound complicated, in practice it's simple. The Major Milestones Plan fits on a single slide that gets rare updates. The Key Decisions Plan gets printed out on a plotter and hung someplace, and it doesn't change much either. The Learning Cycles Plan is the board you create in the Kickoff Event with sticky notes, and the Activity Plans usually end up on whiteboards in someone's office or cubicle.

If you are required to use a project management tool, perhaps to support enterprise reporting requirements, use it for the Key Decisions Plan and leave the rest of the detail out. That should be enough resolution for reports that measure conformance to schedule across an organization. Since your Key Decisions need to be made at the Last Responsible Moment or the program will slip, this plan is the level at which such a conformance metric can help you spot problems early that could affect launch dates.

Status reports are to be avoided at all costs. They communicate nothing of value to your stakeholders and sponsors, because they focus on doing and not learning. Instead, I suggest that you use the status reporting format to discuss the team's active Key Decisions and Knowledge Gaps. Don't report that Dora is running the XYZ experiment, but ran into problems with the centrifuge. Instead, report that Dora is working to understand the optimal concentration of the stabilizer, so the team can finalize the product's formula. This will lead you to talk about the stabilizer options instead of the centrifuge, and that will help you get better feedback from your stakeholders. They might know something about stabilizers that can help you work around the centrifuge problem to eliminate the risk of putting in too little stabilizer.

Obstacle Elimination and Risk Mitigation

Product development is inherently risky, and the most highly prized innovations—the products that will open up new markets or create new product categories—are the most risky of all. In fact, only in a mature market can product developers operate with near certainty that their products will succeed. The Rapid Learning Cycles framework sees risks as obstacles to eliminate, or go around.

Some of the early authors who wrote about Rapid Learning Cycles claimed that, "You cannot move into the Execution Phase until there is no risk." This is a dangerous myth that can wipe out the benefits of the Rapid Learning Cycles framework in one stroke. It certainly does not match the experiences I've had with the teams I've helped. Unless you have a customer with a signed purchase order for your product, there is always risk. In fact, even in that case, you risk that the customer won't like the product and won't buy it again, or that you can't make it.

Product Development Teams Eliminate or Minimize Risk

When a product development program is in its early stages, few Key Decisions have been made, and so the team has a lot of opportunity to minimize risk. The team's focus is on developing knowledge to make good Key Decisions so that the risk is eliminated completely. As the team finalizes Key Decisions, it accumulates the risks that arise from unclosed Knowledge Gaps, and from the need to build imperfect models to close Knowledge Gaps that leave uncertainty in the result. Some Knowledge Gaps, especially those that arise from new markets and new customers, may be nearly impossible to close with accuracy until the product is out into the market.

Other sources of risk include new technology, which isn't proven until it's out in the field; stakeholders such as regulatory bodies that make decisions outside your control; and the product's environment once it leaves your company. I once worked on a product that was experiencing a lot of unexplained failures in one city in India—until people recognized that a local species of mouse found the product to be a perfect nesting box for their babies. Fortunately, that just required us to cover a gap we'd left exposed on the back—an easy fix in the field.

Sometimes the internal environment of the company is a big source of risk: Can the company get the next round of investment? Will the company buy a competitor with a similar product? Is there a restructuring or downsizing on the horizon that will disrupt the project team? Will the strategic focus stay with the product all the way to launch?

Sometimes it's risky to be an innovation program at a company that doesn't understand innovation and has unrealistic expectations. The leaders may not understand the product's strategic fit, all the necessary skills to build the product may not exist inside the company and the product may stress the organization's standard processes for procurement, regulatory approval, intellectual property protection or transfer to manufacturing.

Traditional Risk Management Lowers Risk Visibility

Project Management 101—as represented in a traditional product development program—teaches people to maintain a Risk Management Plan. This is essentially a prioritized list of risks, based on the likelihood that a given risk will occur and the impact of the risk. The Risk Management Plan shows the actions the team will take to reduce or eliminate the risk, and contingency plans in case the risk becomes a reality. The project manager is supposed to create the list and keep it updated. Sometimes teams have a Risk Assessment Checklist to help them find all the risks.

I know there are professional project managers who will disagree with this characterization of traditional risk management, but this is how I've seen it done, if it's been done at all.

In practice, a team may or may not make this plan. If they do, it's often as a pro forma checklist item to make it through a Gate Review. The project manager may or may not update the plan based on what the risk analysis uncovers, and the Risk Management Plan goes somewhere in the team's pile of documentation, never to be seen again.

This is worse than doing nothing, because the team thinks that the project manager has "managed the risks," but in fact the risks have just become invisible. As the project team focuses on the activities that must be done—the deliverables that need to be produced, the suppliers that need to be brought on board and the problems that inevitably crop up—the Risk Management Plan does not address the changes that inevitably arise.

Risk Management Plans Fail to Recognize Change

Every product development team faces the risk that requirements or specifications will change. Our default reaction to this is to demand requirements early and force a "design freeze" on the engineering group. From a risk mitigation perspective, forcing your customers and upstream partners to make decisions earlier is one of the worst things you can do. It only increases the risk that they will make the wrong decision and will need you to change the product design later.

High-impact items with a high likelihood of occurring are not risks. If every one of your last five products has had installation issues and nothing else has changed, "higher than expected installation problems" is not risk—it's a practical certainty. If you have never sold a product through a new sales channel to a new market, then "market risk" fails to express the major obstacles that you face. If you include these near certainties as risks, you dilute your ability to scan the landscape for early warning signs. Even worse, no one spends a lot of time with the Risk Management Plan, and it's possible that the risks it contains will become entirely invisible at exactly the wrong time—when you still have time to do something to mitigate their impact.

Rapid Learning Cycles See Risks as Obstacles to Overcome

Because we have all these risks, we keep learning cycles spinning all the way to product launch. After all the Key Decisions have been made, the focus of the learning cycles changes: now we seek to understand, mitigate and eliminate the biggest risks that could still derail the product. The capacity to do this comes from all of the risk we eliminated earlier in the program by making better Key Decisions.

A team that deeply understands the outstanding risks as it moves into execution is a team that understands the most important work that still needs to be done. Even as the team begins documenting its design decisions, finalizing drawings, validating system prototypes and developing the production process, it never stops eliminating the most important risks. While nothing is 100 percent guaranteed in product development, every risk the team eliminates reduces the likelihood that something will be found that triggers a major program delay.

A team that understands its risks is a team that can recognize when an assumption has proven to be false and a risk has become an issue. It will surface these types of problems much faster than a team with a Risk Management Plan in the documentation pile, and it will be faster to switch to contingency plans and backup strategies. When a risk does materialize, the team will be much better at containing the issue and resolving it quickly. It will seem like a natural extension of the Rapid Learning Cycles process—because it is.

Knowledge Capitalization

Knowledge Capitalization is my term for an organization's capacity to leverage knowledge from one program into another context. When organizations get good at this, incremental product development takes much less time, and innovative solutions are more likely.

Innovative Solutions Rest on a Base of Prior Knowledge

The boundary-pushing areas where people look to find innovation rest upon a solid base of foundational scientific, market and customer knowledge. Biotechnology has accelerated since the Human Genome Project led to advances in DNA sequencing technology. Nanotechnology rests upon the work done at a molecular level to make integrated circuits smaller and smaller. Artificial intelligence leverages algorithms that have been under development since the first theoretical computers in the 1800s and runs on hardware that is so mature that people take it for granted.

Other companies focus more on leveraging customer, market and supply chain knowledge to find innovative ways to expand. Disney is always looking for opportunities to find new ways to entertain families. Proctor & Gamble supports its new product introductions with deep understanding of consumer buying decisions related to household and personal care, and of merchandising in supermarkets.

Many innovations represent combinations of knowledge from unexpected sources. Uber combined the Android and iOS app infrastructure, gateways to facilitate automated payments to contractors and customers' frustrations with traditional taxi service into a new way to get a ride. The iPhone itself combined cellular phone technology with Apple's user design prowess and its iTunes infrastructure for delivering content to build a great product and the ecosystem to support it with apps.

Build–Capture–Share–Use

The cycle of Knowledge Capitalization has four stages:

- **Build.** The knowledge itself must be created and recognized as knowledge. Build–Test–Fix cycles generate a lot of knowledge, but most of it is tacit knowledge built in the minds of the people who went through the cycles, and it's not clear what they learned aside from "here are all the things that didn't work." Well-designed experiments clarify the knowledge that is being built, as it is built.

- **Capture.** Someone must write the knowledge down so that others can use it, and this is not as straightforward as it seems. Product documentation does not readily transfer knowledge because it's difficult for people to see how to shift knowledge from one context to another. Tacit knowledge, the type we get from Build–Test–Fix cycles, is difficult to capture at all. Many organizations have ways to capture technical knowledge or "lessons learned" in some type of system, but it's often too hard to write the reports, or the team tries to do it at the end, when team members are being pulled away on new projects. The Rapid Learning Cycles framework captures knowledge in real time, at the end of every learning cycle. The knowledge capture reports are intentionally quick to complete.

- **Share.** The knowledge must be made accessible to those who can use it. Sometimes IT policies or IP protection rules erect barriers to knowledge sharing, but usually, the systems are the main barrier. Either there is no system at all or the system is too difficult to use. I use the concept of a Knowledge Supermarket to describe the ideal system for knowledge capitalization: it's accessible, allows for tagged searches and browsing within topic areas, makes it easy to add new reports and captures some information about each report to support readers in evaluating its usefulness.

- **Use.** Teams must have powerful incentives to leverage the knowledge that already exists. One would think that teams would seek to avoid the waste of reinvention, because doing so frees up time for more focus on the new areas of a product. But the desire to jump to building something new, Not-Invented-Here syndrome, the inability to recognize useful knowledge out-of-context and difficulties with accessing knowledge make reinvention the path of least resistance all too often.

If any of those phases are missing or malfunctioning, knowledge can't flow from one person or team to another. Of course, knowledge we don't build can't be shared, which is one reason why Build–Test–Fix is so wasteful. And if it's not written down, it can be uncovered only through conversations with the people who have it. If it's written down but not shared, no one can find it to use it. If teams are not encouraged to take the time to investigate prior knowledge, they're likely to just dive into Build–Test–Fix without recognizing when they are in reinvention mode

When organizations have the ability to build knowledge, capture it well, share it with others in their organizations and then incorporate it into products, they can capitalize on that knowledge by accelerating the pace of incremental product development and customizations. They also gain the ability to see solutions to their customers' problems that others can't see, and to recognize opportunities to apply their knowledge to solve new problems for new customers.

The next chapter will describe how we define the opportunity that the new product will capitalize on: the Core Hypothesis.

CHAPTER FIVE

The Core Hypothesis

In Chapter Two, I introduced the concept of the Core Hypothesis—a short statement that encapsulates your vision for this product. You can think of it as your product's "elevator pitch"—the response you would give to an investor or executive that shared a thirty second elevator ride with you.

If you can't distill the core of your product idea down to this statement, it's going to be difficult for your team to stay aligned on your vision.

One Sentence in the Team's Own Words

The Core Hypothesis is a single sentence written in the team's own words. Sponsors and Program Leaders can provide the background information and context that teams need to build the Core Hypothesis, but it's important for the Core Hypothesis to come from the team itself.

The process for writing the Core Hypothesis is much more important than the wording of the sentence itself. This is usually the team's first opportunity to translate the direction they've been given by the team's sponsors into something they can execute. If there are any misunderstandings or misalignments, we see them here first.

Here is an example of a Core Hypothesis:

The HikerPod is a waterproof, dustproof, impact resistant, self-charging fitness armband tailored for trail runners, hikers and backpackers that leverages our expertise in building rugged camera cases into a much larger market.

This is not a charter or a product definition document. It's not even a project brief. Those documents are too detailed and drive too many decisions to be made too quickly. It is a short, memorable statement that describes what your product is.

Before the first quarter of development has passed, your team members should be able to repeat this vision in their sleep. The Core Hypothesis is important because it lets you know when the product has succeeded—when your idea has been proven and when your vision has been realized.

I mentioned earlier that your Core Hypothesis has three dimensions: customer, technical and business. The statement the team writes should emphasize the dimension where you have made the biggest leaps with your idea.

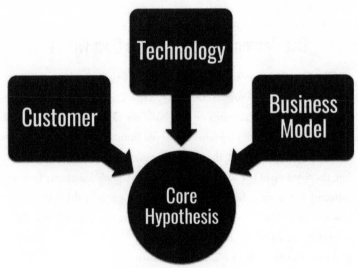

Figure 5.1: The Core Hypothesis

Customer

If you understand the technology well, but the customer is new to you, then the customer will be at the center of your Core Hypothesis. Zappos' Core Hypothesis was that women would buy shoes online if and only if they knew they could return them easily. The mechanics of setting up a website are well known at this point. The impact of an easy return policy and the logistics of managing the outbound and inbound shipments were the biggest unknowns.

To succeed, your product is going to need a clear value proposition that your customers are willing to invest in. Money is relatively easy to invest, compared to time and the learning curve required to change behaviors. Your Core Hypothesis should spell out the riskiest part of the customer interaction you have in mind.

Sometimes the people who purchase a product are not the ones who will use it. Your understanding of the customer needs to include all the links in the customer chain. Resellers, parents, insurance companies, health services and corporate IT groups have needs that are distinct from those of the end users: consumers, children, patients and others.

For HikerPod, the main challenge will be to convince trail runners, hikers and other outdoors adventurers that they need a specialized product to carry their phones out in the wild. Chances are, many of them already have impact-resistant cases or fitness armbands. Why do they need another iPhone case? What if they go on hikes to disconnect from technology? The only way to find out is to talk to a few of them.

Technology

If you understand your customers well but the technology is new, technology will be at the center of your Core Hypothesis. The companies that make sophisticated scientific instruments know their customers well. They know how their customers' budgeting cycles work, how grants and large donations figure into purchasing decisions and which conferences attract the people who are always seeking better instrumentation. The technology that goes into scientific instruments is constantly developing, as companies approach the physical limits of their measurement methods. The question is not, "If we build it, will someone buy it?" Instead, it is, "Can we build it?"

Many innovations use existing technologies in new ways. They may apply a solution in a new industry. They may seek to disrupt an industry with a product that is lower in quality, designed for applications for which a need exists but the mainstream offerings are too expensive. These types of programs have hypotheses embedded in them: that low quality will be cheaper, or that the solution will work under different conditions. Even if all the underlying technologies are well understood, they may not work together the way the team expects.

The HikerPod's Core Hypothesis states that the device will be waterproof, dustproof, impact resistant and solar capable. It may be easy to get all of these features into a device that is also comfortable to wear all day—or it may not be. Unless you already make cell phone cases for the outdoors that have all these features, you just don't know.

Business Model

With many products, the business model is clear: sell products via an established distribution model. For others, it's the center of innovation. Uber and Lyft both seek to disrupt taxi and town car companies by displacing professional drivers with amateurs. They have run into all kinds of difficulties with local regulators and insurance companies. One long, slow learning cycle has centered around background checks for drivers and protection for passengers. The company had to defend itself against a wrongful death suit when an Uber driver killed a six-year-old while off duty but using the Uber app to get business. He had a history of citations for reckless driving on his record. A passenger from India sued the company after her driver assaulted her.

If you are using an established business model that is well understood, you probably don't even need to mention it in your Core Hypothesis. If your intention is to completely change how people buy a product or service, you have some major hypotheses to validate.

In our example, HikerPod will probably be sold in outdoor equipment and running stores and their online counterparts, a business model so common that it's not mentioned. If, however, you are developing this product as an entrepreneur, and you have no experience selling into these stores, you need to validate the hypothesis that the stores will retail the product and buy it from you at a price that enables you to make a profit.

The Core Hypothesis Needs Validation

Your product vision has some Key Decisions embedded in the Core Hypothesis that you have already made, although they should be considered provisional until they are validated. HikerPod's development team needs to validate these assumptions:

- Runners, hikers and others who spend time in the outdoors want their phones to be accessible, protected and charged up.
- Existing products don't provide sufficient accessibility, protection and charging ability.
- It will be waterproof.
- It will be dustproof.
- It will be solar powered.

- We can do all of those things and still price the product competitively.
- It will be sold in places where runners, hikers, etc. will find it.

You can see that some of these hypotheses have both customer and technical implications. It may be hard to engineer solar arrays that meet the requirements for waterproofing and dustproofing. Then again, the customer may not care about these things if solar charging is available.

Some elements of the Core Hypothesis are so fundamental to the product vision that if they are not validated, the program will stop. For HikerPod, you may learn that competitors already offer solutions that are "good enough" and that retailers are not inclined to add another case to their assortment. You may believe that the product is not good unless you can take it on a three-day backpacking trip and use your phone continuously without any other charging device.

Other elements are more flexible. You may not need waterproofing, and the level of impact resistance may not need to be very high. It may be more important to make using the phone easier while in the case.

When you develop your Learning Cycles Plan, it's helpful to treat these hypotheses as Key Decisions with Last Responsible Moments: When do you need to know that HikerPod will be waterproof, and how it will be waterproofed? When do you need to know who your first retailers will be?

Changes to the Core Hypothesis

The Core Hypothesis may never change over the life of a program, but when it does change, this needs to be recognized as a significant shift in the team's direction that requires sponsor buy-in. The Core Hypothesis always reflects the current state of the program. As Program Leader, you are responsible for recognizing when new information or new direction from your sponsor indicates the need to update the Core Hypothesis.

We normally recognize this need at an Integration Event, when a Key Decision must be made that is not in alignment with the current Core Hypothesis. Perhaps one of the assumptions in the Core Hypothesis has been disproven, or the company has changed strategy.

Since your sponsors and stakeholders are in the Integration Event with you, this is the easiest time to discuss the impact of the Key Decision on the Core Hypothesis and make whatever adjustments need to be made.

Core Hypotheses may also change at Gate Reviews where the team may not be present. If so, it's important to work with the team to finalize the updates to the Core Hypothesis, rather than making them without the team. The team should feel strong ownership for this statement and they will resent any changes that take place without giving them time to interpret and express the changes in their own words.

When you have your Core Hypothesis, you can begin to think about what it's going to take to bring your vision to life. It's time to start planning.

In the next chapter, we will dive into the first major aspect of the Rapid Learning Cycles framework: Key Decisions.

CHAPTER SIX

Key Decisions

The Rapid Learning Cycles framework is built around the theory that when we learn what we need to learn to make good decisions and we make them at the right time, we won't have to revisit them later, when it's expensive, time-consuming and painful to change them, and that good decisions made at the right time will help us deliver the product faster.

The next three chapters walk you through the process of developing the Learning Cycles Plan. We build the plan at a Kickoff Event, where the team defines its Key Decisions, Knowledge Gaps and cadences. Then the team compiles those decisions into a Learning Cycles Plan that describes how the team will organize its knowledge creation into learning cycles. By the end of this event, your team will have established the Rapid Learning Cycles framework for your program and will be prepared to come in the next day and start learning.

Your first task to establish Rapid Learning Cycles is to discover what you need to learn the most: the Key Decisions that have both a major impact on your program's success and a lot of Knowledge Gaps to close in order to make them with confidence.

The time taken to define Key Decisions helps the team focus on the most important Knowledge Gaps. The timing for these Key Decisions determines the amount of time that the team has for closing Knowledge Gaps and their relative priority. The amount of uncertainty that remains when a Key Decision must be made determines the amount of risk that the program team carries forward if they cannot close the Knowledge Gaps.

What Is a Key Decision?

A Key Decision is any significant decision that the team must make in the context of the product development program that is high impact and has high unknowns.

Since product developers make thousands of decisions over the life of a product development program, it's not possible to give every decision the same level of attention if you want to get your product to market in a reasonable time. Instead, we look for those decisions that tend to get revisited later in the project, with strong ripple effects for the program as a whole when they change. No team has unlimited time and money. It's much better for a team to go deeply into a few areas that have a lot of risk than to superficially address everything.

If a minor, isolated decision is wrong, fixing the defect is relatively easy. But if the team makes a fundamental error in the logic behind the system architecture, the market conditions, the regulatory landscape or the cost structure, the project could be delayed and even canceled late in the program. The mission of the Rapid Learning Cycles framework is to ensure that this doesn't happen.

Here are four criteria to help you filter out the high-impact Key Decisions from the ones that are merely important:

- **High impact on the product's success.** Key Decisions make a big difference in whether or not the company can sell enough of the product at a profitable price. If the decision is wrong, everyone will know and the entire program will be at risk. It may seem as though every decision has this level of significance, but after a few learning cycles, you will know where that is true and where it just seems that way.

- **High cost of change if it must be revisited later.** Key Decisions lead to investments of time or money that are expensive to undo: supplier contracts get signed, key design elements get finalized, customer expectations get set. If the team must revisit the decisions later, the cost of change can be so high that the business model no longer makes sense.

- **Required to deliver the product.** Key Decisions must be made at some point in time or the product cannot go forward. If the decision gets delayed past this point, the entire product will be delayed. A decision to incorporate an extra feature is usually not a Key Decision.

- **Drives other decisions.** Key Decisions drive other decisions, large and small. They tend to reside at the architecture or business model level, rather than in the detailed design. This is why they cause so many problems when they are not decided correctly: changing the decision may require touching every subsystem, and every individual change introduces more risk into the program.

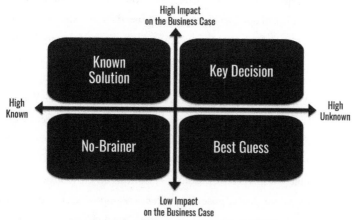

Figure 6.1: Not Every Decision Is a Key Decision

Key Decisions also have high unknowns. This is a decision that you cannot make today unless you are willing to bet your product on a guess. You do not have the knowledge you need to make the decision with confidence. If you will build this knowledge in the natural course of development, and the knowledge comes in time to inform the decision, the decision is probably not a Key Decision. Key Decisions have significant Knowledge Gaps that the team needs to close in order to make the decision without guesswork.

Key Decisions Are Focused Questions with Choices

We've learned that teams get more benefit from the Rapid Learning Cycles framework when they ask good questions and recognize the distinction between Key Decisions, Knowledge Gaps, activities and deliverables.

We define both Key Decisions and Knowledge Gaps in the form of well-formulated questions with these characteristics:

- **Focused.** A well-formulated question is focused. You want to be able to make a crisp decision. It's difficult to make a decision if the question is vague, too broad or overly constrained. A question that is too open will lead to time wasted on knowledge that does not contribute to this product—or any product. A question that is too constrained will lead to knowledge about this product, but not the product next in line on the roadmap.

- **Answerable.** A well-formulated question has an answer. You may not like the answer very much or you may have difficulty getting the answer. Nevertheless, the question has an answer. The answers to Key Decision questions come from the people responsible for making the decisions—the decision is the answer.

- **Does not presuppose an answer.** Presuppositions come with a lot of untested assumptions built in. "Shall we use aluminum for our frame?" is a question that presupposes an answer. Instead, we set our assumptions aside to find the best answer to the question—not just for now, but for the future: "What material will we use for our frames?" Open-ended questions drive us to explore alternatives and understand the design space more thoroughly.

A Key Decision always represents a choice. The answer to the question is a decision that someone will make. The decision maker can be someone on the team, the team as a group or a stakeholder. The questions often have the form, "What **will** we . . . ?"

Deliverables are bundles of decisions. They sometimes have Key Decisions embedded within them. "What will be the requirements?" is not a Key Decision. The requirements document is a deliverable that captures both Key Decisions and many other decisions that are not high impact or that are well-known.

Key Decisions are not just for the technical team. These questions can come from anywhere that the work of product development gets done.

Key Decisions Can Come from Anywhere

Engineers often find that it's easy to see Key Decisions that arise from technical Knowledge Gaps, but Key Decisions can also arise from business models, including the targeted customer base, pricing and revenue generation, use cases and channel strategies. In fact, if the technology is well understood, these may be the most important Key Decisions you have.

For this reason, there is no standard list of Key Decisions that any company can define. Key Decisions change from program to program, depending upon what's new or different about the product and how effective your knowledge sharing has been on previous programs. For example, the decision to use a new motor may be straightforward if you use a supplier that you know well and the motor design is mature. But if you are trying to push the limits on performance, you may have a lot of Key Decisions related to the motor design.

Figure 6.2: Sources of Key Decisions

In fact, it's helpful to recognize that if the team captures the knowledge it builds, today's Key Decisions become tomorrow's known solutions—future teams won't have to close the decision's Knowledge Gaps again.

Some teams can pinpoint their Key Decisions quickly and easily: they have a new subsystem design, a new material or a new supplier that's adding risk to the project. Other teams may have a difficult time figuring out where their Key Decisions are, especially if the team is small and lacks basic functional knowledge, such as a marketing-based Innovation Team without good technical support or an Advanced R&D team without marketing support.

In the previous chapter, I mentioned that your Core Hypothesis contains some embedded Key Decisions you have already made provisionally. What elements of your Core Hypothesis are the most uncertain? Which ones do you have good data to support, and which ones represent your best guess? These provisional decisions need to go on the list so that the team can validate them.

To make it even more complicated, your functional partners also have Key Decisions to make. The procurement group needs to qualify and select suppliers for critical parts. Manufacturing may need to figure out exactly where it will make a given product. Sales may need to understand how to position this product vs. the competition for customers that are mostly focused on price.

Chances are your first list of candidates for Key Decisions will be long. You need to find the critical few that are worth the investment in early learning.

Find the Candidate Key Decisions

To find your first-pass list of Key Decisions, review the Core Hypothesis and high-level project schedule, if there is one, with the team. That will help set the context for uncovering Key Decisions.

Then break the team into a few small groups and ask them to brainstorm key decisions on a specific area of the project. Work with subteams if you have them; if not, group related functional partners together. Then give them a pile of sticky notes, good markers and no more than thirty minutes of time. That will be enough to jump-start the process.

When brainstorming Key Decisions, consider focusing your team on just the next phase of development, whatever that is. In Concept Evaluation, the Key Decisions may all arise from the need to get preliminary validation for the Core Hypothesis in order to justify the investment to develop the product. In later phases, the Key Decisions will be driven by the need to prove feasibility, establish the product architecture and refine the business case.

When your team reaches the next phase, you will have much more experience to draw from to help you find the Key Decisions that will be most important when you get there. Until then, consider keeping any obvious Key Decisions in a "parking area" until you're ready for them so that they don't get lost but the team stays focused.

The Critical Few Key Decisions

I can't tell you how many Key Decisions you should have without taking some time to get to know your product idea. It helps to remember that the reason we use the Rapid Learning Cycles framework is to make better decisions that stick, so that the team can get from idea to launch as quickly and smoothly as possible.

Which of the decisions on your list have to hold, or else the team will be forced into a major reset? Which ones will benefit the most from a little bit of investigation to reduce the risk of a late change, even if the risk can't be eliminated entirely? Which of these decisions keep you up at night?

We pay close attention to Key Decisions that involve the aspects of the product that are new to us and therefore introduce the greatest amount of risk. If this is a line extension to bring a product to a new price point or market segment, that's where the Key Decisions will be. If it's an attempt to leapfrog a competitor's performance in an existing product line with an established market, the Key Decisions will be the ones that drive performance improvement. If this is a new app based on existing platforms but that solves a customer problem in a novel way, your Key Decisions will be focused on use cases, user experience and revenue-generation models.

Other Key Decisions can go lower on the list. Which ones are more flexible and easier to change? Which ones will be inconvenient to change but not disruptive? Which ones are perhaps better made provisionally and then reviewed in the next version, after we see how users react? Which ones can we learn about opportunistically—if we have time?

You probably have a lot of decisions that are important but not key. For example, the decision about where to manufacture a product is an important one, but if the development process is similar, the manufacturing partners are people you've worked with on previous products and the decision gets made on time, it's not a Key Decision. You may have decisions that are dependent upon Key Decisions but have no independent Knowledge Gaps. These are also not Key Decisions, since you will have the knowledge to make them when it's time.

This is also the time to look for Key Decisions that are bundles of decisions. "Who will we choose as our suppliers?" encompasses many decisions. It's better to break out the suppliers separately. Some suppliers you know well, and you also may need new suppliers you haven't yet found for components that are new to you. Suppliers you know are known solutions; suppliers you need to find are Key Decisions if they are not easy to find and/or difficult to switch out later in the program.

Knowledge Gaps are not Key Decisions. For example, you may not know how a regulatory agency will react to your product and what your regulatory strategy will be. But you will have a regulatory strategy and achieve compliance in the markets where you choose to sell the product; not registering the product is not an option. You may have a Knowledge Gap such as, "What are the applicable regulations for this product in our target markets?" You'll just learn what you need to do and then do it—there is not a choice to be made.

Focus Key Decisions on the Next Major Milestone

If you're working in a corporate R&D group, you probably already know how long you have to spend in the next phase before you are expected to reach the next major milestone: an approved concept, a business case, a functional prototype or a production process. Your PDP calls out the deliverables (bundles of decisions) that the team needs to complete in order to get through the next phase.

Most of the Key Decisions for this phase are probably buried in those deliverables. Focus on Key Decisions that relate to deliverables for future phases only for items with long lead times.

If you're doing this on your own or you have no guidelines, then set your next major milestone. Set a target date to reach it that feels like a bit of a stretch—maybe 10 percent less than you think you need to get to there. Your milestone could be a first-pass business case and pitch for investors, a working prototype or even the Minimum Viable Product.

Once we have identified a Key Decision and validated that it is a choice that will have high impact and that has a lot of unknowns, we keep it on the plan. We don't remove Key Decisions for reasons related to time. Instead, we prioritize the Knowledge Gaps that underlie the Key Decisions and recognize that not all Knowledge Gaps will close.

This means that some Key Decisions will need to be made without all the knowledge we'd like to have. Since Key Decisions are, by definition, important to get right, the missing knowledge puts the decision at risk, and the risk is important enough to manage. It's easier to understand this risk if we see how the Key Decisions fit together to lead to the next major milestone.

Key Decisions in Sequence

Key Decisions have a natural sequence because some decisions depend upon other decisions. Now that you have the critical few Key Decisions, the next step is to find the sequence. In a Kickoff Event, we use sticky notes to visualize the flow of Key Decisions. The first-pass sequence should have no dates at all—it should model the dependencies between one Key Decision and the next. When you finish this step, you have the second level of the Multilevel Plan. After you've built the Learning Cycles Plan, you'll be able to add the time dimension to produce this Key Decisions Plan.

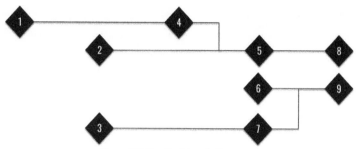

Figure 6.3: Key Decisions in Sequence

You may find that you are already late. That's good information that most teams don't get until they are a lot further down the road. This knowledge will help you understand how to prioritize your team's work. If time to market is not critical to the product's success, perhaps you can get more time. But usually this motivates the team to get smart about learning quickly and making good decisions so that they can get the product out on time.

You may also find that some decisions are being made too early: they are being made before the Last Responsible Moment.

The Last Responsible Moment

The Last Responsible Moment is the last point in time when you can make a decision without significant impacts on downstream partners. It is the last point in time that a decision must be made. This means that the decision must not be subject to any additional sign-offs, review meetings or executive oversight. All of that has to take place before this date, so that the decision is truly final. All the parties involved in making the decision should come to the decision meeting prepared to make the decision.

Everyone who needs to participate in making the decision needs to be there, or to send word that they will support the decision that is made without them. After the Last Responsible Moment, it's too late to challenge the decision or bring it up for debate. As the Program Leader, you need to consider how you will reinforce this, so that other stakeholders understand that changes after this point will hurt the product.

How do you know when delaying or revisiting a decision will hurt the product? By asking yourself what will happen. If it will delay the program—or cause a downstream partner in Marketing or Operations to scramble and take shortcuts—then you are there. But if it just means that someone downstream won't get the decision when they want it (as opposed to when they need it) then you may want to consider challenging the date to see if it actually the Last Responsible Moment.

If change continues to be easy for your partners, you are not yet at the Last Responsible Moment. If they force the decision now, instead of waiting a little longer, fixing things will be much more inconvenient. The more time you have, the less likely you are to need to revisit a decision when change is painful.

One indicator of the Last Responsible Moment is the cost of change. It should go up dramatically after the Last Responsible Moment. If it doesn't, you are not there yet. Last Responsible Moments usually line up with things like lead times to place orders with key suppliers, get tools built and installed, or deliver final copy for translation and localization. If you can find a way to reduce those lead times, you can delay the Last Responsible Moment.

You can extend the Last Responsible Moment, giving yourselves more time to close Knowledge Gaps, by helping your downstream partners to:

- **Work with partial information.** Find out what exactly your downstream partners need to take their next steps, and then give them only that information. For example, your supply chain partner probably does not need to know the final geometry down to the last millimeter in order to know how much raw material it will take to make something.

- **Work within the set of decisions that has already been communicated.** For working with industrial designers and others, it's helpful to define an "envelope" that represents the maximum dimensions that the mechanism will need. As long as the envelope is not exceeded, the industrial designers can manipulate the external form of the product and its packaging without waiting for the mechanism itself to be finalized.

You may also need to consider whether you need to help them by:

- **Defining integration points early, but let the subsystem interiors retain their freedom longer.** This keeps other subsystems from being held up or going through multiple loops of changes in the places where they have to connect. The interfaces have early Last Responsible Moments, but the inner workings of the subsystems can have much later ones.

- **Spending money to decrease lead times.** Sometimes it will be worth the money to pay for expedited processing rather than forcing a decision that has a big unclosed Knowledge Gap. Sometimes the extra cost of delaying the decision is much less than the cost of changing it later.

- **Working with downstream partners to make the interface more efficient.** If downstream partners have put a lot of buffer into their processes because you are difficult for them to work with, you can help them remove it. If your documentation is confusing or incomplete and there are a lot of changes, do what you can to build a more collaborative relationship. Once they are more assured that you are giving them what they need, they won't feel compelled to demand things early to allow for miscommunication.

Every decision has its own Last Responsible Moment. Traditional product development programs often have a "design freeze" date, after which changes must go through an approval process. But that date is probably too late for some design decisions, and too early for others. It might be difficult to change the PC board or the layout of the keypad after a given date, but changing the color of the injection-molded buttons could be possible for weeks afterward. It doesn't make sense to try to learn everything simultaneously so that the group can lock down all of its decisions for an artificial deadline. Instead, we assign each Key Decision to its own Last Responsible Moment.

Find the Last Responsible Moment for Your Key Decisions

To finalize the sequence, move decisions forward to their true Last Responsible Moments. For each Key Decision, ask your team when the decision needs to be made before the cost of changing it goes up dramatically, or when not having the decision will cause the product to be delayed. Consider when these decisions have been made on other programs and the impact of changing them. Ask if there is anything you can do to delay the Last Responsible Moment.

You may notice two things about this sequence of decisions. First, it will direct you to spend more time in up-front development, especially if you are working within your company's Product Development Process. You may need as much as 30 percent more time in early development.

You may also see that you don't have enough time to do any learning before some of your first Key Decisions are due. You may find that you are already past the Last Responsible Moment to make some of your Key Decisions, and that these Key Decisions have Knowledge Gaps. These will be the Knowledge Gaps that go to the top of your priority list in your Learning Cycles Plan. If you have a lot of these, you have two options:

- **If the next milestone does not have a hard date already, you can set the date now based on what you've learned.** It will probably be later than you would like, or than you believe your leadership team will accept. But if your company's products are always late to market, chances are your product will be done faster than the typical program. Your dates are more likely to hold once you account for schedule delays. Always compare your expected launch dates to typical products done the normal way—not to product deadlines that no one meets.

- **If you already have a milestone that is tied to a major customer pull event, look for safe options.** If you have a trade show, budgeting cycles, or seasonal market windows dictating your launch date, then you need to reduce the risk of missing the date. For example, you can drop some of the features you expected to deliver to eliminate the Key Decisions and Knowledge Gaps involving those features, or you can use proven technology for some part of the product to focus the team on the part that is truly new.

As Program Leader, you must not allow managers and other stakeholders to overrule the schedule. Their tendency will be to tell you to spend less time learning, but this is exactly the approach that gets the results that your company typically gets. Why would you want to do that? Consider the options available to you to help you defend the schedule, especially the time you have allocated for learning. If they insist, remove buffer from later in the program.

The last step is to establish owners and Integration Events for your Key Decisions.

Key Decisions Have Owners

Someone is responsible for making a Key Decision, but that does not get the team off the hook. The Rapid Learning Cycles framework requires teams to supply the decision makers with the knowledge they need to make good Key Decisions. This is not the kind of program where Marketing writes specs that Engineering implements without question.

The Rapid Learning Cycles team collaborates to develop the best product. The business owners work with the technical staff to establish the right features, performance and quality specs and design in a conversation: "Here's what we need." "Here's what we can do." "Great; can we do A?" "Not easily. We can do B a lot faster, and that would give us time to do C and D, too." "How about B, C and F?" "We can do that." "Make it so."

The owners are responsible for making Key Decisions at the Last Responsible Moment—not later and not earlier. The team is responsible for prioritizing its work to give the Key Decision owners the best available information to make that decision.

If you have any major decisions that will be made outside the team, you will need to get engaged with those stakeholders to help them understand the Last Responsible Moment and the impact on the overall program if the decision gets delayed. For example, you may need to know where the product will be manufactured in order to effectively model the cost of goods sold (COGS) for your product and design tools that will work in the chosen location. If you cannot get a good decision on this, your COGS models may be off and your tool designs will be delayed.

It will take some leadership from you to help your stakeholders make decisions within this framework. They may be asked to delay their decisions until much later than they believe they should. They may need help to break down their Key Decisions into the Knowledge Gaps that your team needs to close for them. They may not make data-driven decisions at all, and may need your help to process the knowledge that the team has built for them. The Integration Events will reinforce the decision making you need from them.

Align Key Decisions with Integration Events

As much as possible, you want to group Key Decisions into Integration Events. The benefits of making decisions with all the stakeholders in the room, without having to call a meeting for every decision, outweighs the impact of moving the Last Responsible Moments around a little bit. You especially want to coordinate decisions that have a lot of downstream impact, because you will want to get your partners into the room with you and share what you've learned with them. Even if they have no say in the decisions themselves, they will be able to execute the decisions better if they understand the rationale for them.

A few Key Decisions may be made between the meetings, especially if those Key Decisions relate to a specific subsystem or function. If a Key Decision involves just a handful of team members, there is no need to wait for an Integration Event to make that decision. But the decision owners do need to be prepared to report on it at the next Integration Event so that everyone knows that the decision was made.

You don't want to combine Gate Reviews with Integration Events. Gate Reviews are management control points for leaders—who are not normally part of the program team—to review the program, give feedback and determine whether or not the product still has a viable business case. Instead, first conduct the Integration Event, where you make Key Decisions. Then have the Gate Review a week or two later, while the decisions and the rationale are fresh in the minds of the people participating in the review. This discourages senior leaders from trying to "help" on decisions where they don't have all the background knowledge to assist the team in making a good decision.

I'll establish the Integration Events as part of building the Learning Cycles Plan in Chapter Eight, and then describe how to run an Integration Event in Chapter Nine.

Before we get there, we need to define, prioritize and select the first Knowledge Gaps.

CHAPTER SEVEN

Knowledge Gaps

Now that you have your Key Decisions, the next step is to build the plan to close the Knowledge Gaps so that you learn what you need to learn to make the Key Decisions when you need to make them. You'll also scan the program landscape to see if there are any other critical Knowledge Gaps you need to close.

In the Learning Phases of the program, team members will spend their time doing the work to close Knowledge Gaps. As the program moves into the Execution Phases, the team will have less and less time for learning but it does not completely go away until the product launches. Even at the very end of the program, the team may encounter situations where a little bit of learning leads to a much better product.

What Is a Knowledge Gap?

A Knowledge Gap is something that we don't know today, but that we need to know in order to deliver the product.

We formulate a Knowledge Gap in the form of a question with an answer. We may not be able to get the answer easily, but it does exist. For example, I can't tell you how many great white sharks there are in the wild, but that number exists. Someone somewhere has probably done a study

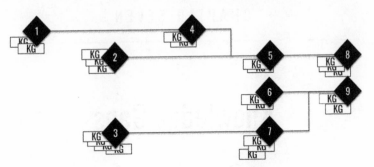

Figure 7.1: Key Decisions Have Knowledge Gaps

to give an approximation of the answer that may or may not be good enough to meet our needs. Knowledge Gap questions seek to answer questions like, "What can we do?" "What are the viable alternatives?" "What is the evidence that we need to support our decision?" "What does the evidence say?"

Any product development program starts out with many Knowledge Gaps, and you will never be able to close them all.

As the Program Leader, you will need to help your team accept this: the team will always have more Knowledge Gaps than it can close. Your team members will find that Knowledge Gaps tend to multiply: closing one Knowledge Gap may lead to three or four new ones. A team that tries to close every single Knowledge Gap to deliver the perfect product is a team that is setting itself up for failure. Instead, you choose which Knowledge Gaps to close within a learning cycle from a prioritized backlog of all the Knowledge Gaps your team could close. Then you replan them at every Learning Cycle Event so that the team is always working on the ones that are most important to the program.

In a traditional product development program, the team also seeks to close some Knowledge Gaps because otherwise it would not be able to produce the deliverables for the next milestone. But the team members' focus is on doing instead of learning, and so they would not seek the fastest, cheapest way to learn. They work in Build–Test–Fix cycles even for things that are better learned via research or experimentation. They may work to close low-impact but easy Knowledge Gaps, leaving the high-impact but difficult ones until there is no time to close them. Some Knowledge Gaps may remain entirely hidden until the time comes to make a Key Decision and the team discovers it doesn't know what it needs to know.

The Rapid Learning Cycles framework seeks to expose these challenges early. Even if your program has a lot of Knowledge Gaps that cannot be easily closed, the team still exits the Learning Phases in a much better place than the typical development team. Your team has had some time to discover and map out many of the "unknown unknowns" that tend to kill projects. Your goal will never be to reach 100 percent success assured—as if that were possible. Your goal is to understand the risks you take—and prepare to take action if a risk materializes. Even a little time spent trying to close an important Knowledge Gap will help your team understand the risk of proceeding without the knowledge.

The good news is that you already know that you don't know—that you were forced to make a decision that has uncertainty. You are much less likely to be surprised, because you'll know what the early warning signs are: an assumption that didn't check out or a predictable side effect that arises. The Rapid Learning Cycles framework is not intended to eliminate all obstacles between you and your new product. It will prevent a lot of problems, and reduce the severity of the problems that do arise. This is why we make a comprehensive list of Knowledge Gaps, even though we know we cannot close them all.

The Comprehensive Set of Knowledge Gaps

We use a combination of methods that help us look at the product from a number of different perspectives to build the comprehensive set of

Knowledge Gaps. Then we bring in other people who have some distance from the program, to help us find the things we are too close to see.

The Knowledge Gaps you need to close to make the Key Decisions are easy to find. You may also have some Knowledge Gaps you need to close before you can prepare other deliverables, such as regulatory filings. These "known unknowns" are also usually the easiest ones to close.

To start, list all the Knowledge Gaps associated with every Key Decision you have identified. Then brainstorm as a team to find any other big Knowledge Gaps. You might ask the team, "What else do we need to learn to build a working prototype?" or "What else do we need to learn to solidify the business model?" If this product is based on an existing product, ask, "What's different? What's new?"

The goal is to pull together every Knowledge Gap that the team members have in their heads, and to get them out where everyone can see them. Every team member has specific Knowledge Gaps that concern him or her the most—the ones that keep them up at night. Once team members see their most important Knowledge Gap in writing, they'll relax, making it easier for them to see other Knowledge Gaps. The team members will feed off of each other to add to the list of overall Knowledge Gaps.

After the team members have come up with everything they can on their own, it's time for them to look at other programs for a new perspective. It's especially helpful for the team to ask itself, "What problems have other teams like ours encountered?" You can look at past projects' Risk Management Plans, failure points, late design loopbacks and Engineering Change Requests to see if there are patterns that might recur for your product. You can look at the problems you see in competitors' products—the compromises they were forced to make.

Finally, it's helpful to get an expert set of eyes from someone outside the team. This is not a management review or approval. Instead, it is an opportunity to get perspective from someone who is not as close to the project. These reviewers should ask themselves, "What's missing?"

A simple way to get this review is to invite one or two outside experts to attend the team's Kickoff Event. They participate in the group exercises to identify Key Decisions and Knowledge Gaps, asking questions and challenging the team's assumptions about what it already knows. In my experience, teams appreciate this kind of help, which feels more like collaboration than criticism.

If you have major Key Decisions to make regarding the business model, you may need experts from Marketing and Finance. It's a good idea to solicit input from Operations, Manufacturing or Supply Chain partners here, too.

You will emerge from this step with a large stack of Knowledge Gaps that need to be prioritized.

Rating Knowledge Gaps for Prioritization

Once you have a comprehensive set of Knowledge Gaps, the next step is to put together a prioritized list. This is the most important step in the Kickoff Event because it leads the team to build a Learning Cycles Plan that maximizes the value of the time the team has to learn.

We prioritize Knowledge Gaps based on three factors:

- **Criticality.** How important is it to the program that you close this Knowledge Gap? How much risk is there that the related Key Decisions will be wrong if this Knowledge Gap is not closed? What is the impact on the program? Key Decisions are high impact by definition, but not all of the related Knowledge Gaps contribute to the impact to the same degree.

- **Duration.** How long do you think you will need to close the Knowledge Gap? It's important to scale this factor to the team's resource levels. If everyone on the team is allocated to this project at 30%, it may take three times as long to close Knowledge Gaps.

- **Uncertainty of Duration.** How certain are you that your duration estimate is accurate? If this is something you know how to do, your certainty is high and so your uncertainty is low. If this is something you've never done before, your uncertainty is high.

We assign a rating for each of the three factors to the Knowledge Gap. I like to use a five-point scale for the factors—that seems to give enough granularity without prolonging arguments.

I don't believe in quantitative ranking of Knowledge Gaps. When a team is new to the Rapid Learning Cycles framework, its members don't know how long it takes to close Knowledge Gaps. Their ratings of the factors are not calibrated with each other. A lot of subjectivity goes into assigning the numbers. A numerical score provides the team with a false sense of certainty about their prioritization list that leads them to work on the wrong things first.

I find that it's best for teams to just use the factors as a guide without trying to calculate an overall "prioritization score." The value of assigning ratings to the factors comes out of the discussion that takes place as the team weighs the Knowledge Gaps against each other.

If many of your Knowledge Gaps have long durations, consider breaking them apart into smaller Knowledge Gaps. For example, "How does the candidate molecule perform in a mouse model?" is a Knowledge Gap that would probably rank as a "5" on Duration and take many learning cycles to close. If the team manages it as one large Knowledge Gap, then the team members will give status updates—but they won't necessarily report what they have learned so far. To get better visibility, the team can break it apart into three smaller ones:

- What is the experimental design for our mouse model? (Work with your mouse experts to design a good experiment.)
- What are our preliminary observations from running the experiment? (Could we get enough mice or get enough of the molecule? Could we give it to the mice without killing them immediately?

What did we seen when we monitored their health during the trial? Did we get good data?)

- How does the candidate molecule perform in a mouse model? (Results analysis.)

The team working on the mouse model would have significant progress to report—and Knowledge Gaps that have been closed—in at least every other learning cycle over the months it takes to run an experiment with mice. If something goes wrong with the experimental design or the experiment itself, the team will learn about it faster than if it has to wait for final results before it hears anything.

When all of the Knowledge Gaps have been rated, every Knowledge Gap will have ratings for Criticality, Duration and Uncertainty of Duration. The next step is to sort them into categories that will help us place them on the Learning Cycles Plan.

Categories of Knowledge Gaps to Plan

The next step is to sort the Knowledge Gaps into categories that we'll use for building the Learning Cycles Plan. We sort the Knowledge Gaps into these categories:

- **Do Now.** Knowledge Gaps with high criticality but low duration and low uncertainty of duration. These quick wins help the team build momentum. They may settle questions that eliminate other Knowledge Gaps that would take longer to close.
- **Do Next.** Knowledge Gaps with high criticality, duration and uncertainty of duration. Since you don't know how long they will take but they must be closed, you start on them early.
- **Prioritize.** Knowledge Gaps with high criticality that are not in the first two categories. You place the remaining high critical-

ity Knowledge Gaps on the plan before any others with lower criticality.

- **Do If Time.** All Knowledge Gaps with medium and low criticality, low duration and low uncertainty of duration. You'll use these to fill out the plan, but they will also be the first ones removed if the team is overloaded.

- **Do Not Close.** All low criticality Knowledge Gaps that cannot be closed quickly. They have medium to high duration and/or uncertainty of duration. They are not worth the team's time and so you admit now that you will not close them.

This sequence helps the team avoid the traps of closing the easy things without regard to priority first, or of trying to close every Knowledge Gap for early Key Decisions when the team needs to start working on high criticality Knowledge Gaps for later decisions that will take a long time to close.

Now that the Knowledge Gaps have been categorized, the team is ready to start building its Learning Cycles Plan.

CHAPTER EIGHT

Cadence and the Learning Cycles Plan

Now that you have your Key Decisions and Knowledge Gaps, the next step is to build the plan to close the Knowledge Gaps so that you learn what you need to learn to make the Key Decisions when you need to make them.

Learning Cycle Cadence

Before you can build the plan, you need to establish the cadence of learning cycles. Now that the team understands the Knowledge Gaps, it is prepared to decide how long one learning cycle will be for the program. When your organization begins to use Rapid Learning Cycles on every program, it may need to standardize and align cadences in order to support team members who are on multiple programs. If you are running a pilot program or you have a dedicated team, then your team will set a cadence for itself.

In Chapter Three, I mentioned that the learning cycle cadence usually falls between two and eight weeks, with four weeks being the most common choice. The Knowledge Gaps will tell you how long the learning cycles should be. If you are in Concept Evaluation and you have a lot of

Knowledge Gaps that require things like customer interviews, literature research or small-scale experimentation, you can turn fast cycles. If you are in Late Feasibility / Early Detailed Design, and you are already working with suppliers to make full-scale prototypes, you probably need longer learning cycles.

The cadence you choose should feel a little fast—but not so fast that no one has anything to report at the first Learning Cycle Event. Some Knowledge Gaps may need to stretch across multiple learning cycles, but the ones you rated in the middle of the duration scale should fit into one cycle on your Learning Cycles Plan.

This is also a good time for the team to decide how often it wants to have Status Events (daily, weekly, biweekly) and the timing of Integration Events.

The Right Cadence for Your Project

Establish your team's learning cycle cadence first, and then build the rest of the program around that.

This learning cycle cadence is fixed. Our experience shows that teams that have experimented with variable lengths for their learning cycles (changing the length of the learning cycle for every cycle) do not realize all of the benefits of using the Rapid Learning Cycles framework because they are not learning faster.

Your team should have enough time in each learning cycle to learn something meaningful and close some Knowledge Gaps. When you get together at the end of the cycle, you should have some results to share.

You will establish cadence by number of weeks rather than months (that is, every fourth Friday, not the fourth Friday of the month). If you use months, the team has an unsteady cadence. Every few months, the team has an extra week. That's basically a week of wasted work, since the Knowledge Gaps are scaled to learning cycles.

But the learning cycles should be short enough that the team gets together often and does not have time to drift apart. The cadence should feel a bit fast at first. It should challenge the team to come up with faster experiments and creative ways to close Knowledge Gaps.

In general, the faster you can build models and test them, the shorter your learning cycles should be. You can adjust the cadence at the end of a learning cycle—but only if it's clear that the cycle you've chosen is not the right one or if the program has moved into a new phase. It's easier to lengthen a cycle that's too short than it is to shorten a cycle that's too long. I will discuss how to recognize this issue and fix it in Chapter Fourteen.

Idea investigation projects should operate on very short cycles—two to four weeks. As the idea matures, these cycles can get longer. It's easiest to switch cadences when the team reaches a major milestone or expands to add additional functional groups. If you have a phase gate lifecycle, a gate is often a good opportunity to revisit the cadence.

When your program has the right cadence, you'll know. You'll feel the rhythm internally, and you'll be able to see external evidence that it's taking hold in the plans that people make for their learning cycles.

The Timing of Integration Events

Once you have your cadence, you can decide when to hold Integration Events. These events always take place at the end of a learning cycle, alongside a Learning Cycle Event.

A few teams have experimented with Integration Events that took place in the middle of a learning cycle. This proved to be so disruptive that the value of improving the timing for Key Decisions was outweighed by the loss of productivity for the rest of the program.

Integration Events don't need a regular cadence. Teams often find that they need an Integration Event right after the first learning cycle to make some quick decisions that will guide the direction of the program. They also need an Integration Event one learning cycle before they reach their next major milestone to finalize decisions that need to be made to complete the deliverables for that milestone.

In between, they may choose to hold an Integration Event after every two or three learning cycles, or even after every learning cycle in a program that is moving fast. Teams that go more than one quarter (twelve weeks) without an Integration Event seem to lose contact with their stakeholders' needs, so it's better to schedule an Integration Event at least that often.

I've said that you make decisions at the Last Responsible Moment, and that you make Key Decisions at Integration Events. In practice, teams usually find that clusters of Key Decisions need to be made at nearly the same time, and these are natural focal points for Integration Events. In the context of the overall program, we've learned that it makes more sense to pull up or delay a Key Decision by a week or two in order to align it with an Integration Event, rather than forcing the team to operate out of step with its learning cycle cadence.

If one Key Decision needs to be made before another Key Decision, a team can make the Key Decisions at the same event, as long as the sequence of Key Decisions within the event allows for this.

The Learning Cycles Plan

The final step is to turn all you've done into a Learning Cycles Plan, with Knowledge Gaps assigned to specific learning cycles. The easiest way to do this in the Kickoff Event is to cover a section of wall 2 meters high by 2 to 4 meters long with paper, and draw a grid on it. You can also use a large whiteboard.

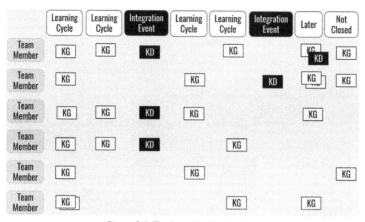

Figure 8.1: The Learning Cycles Plan

As described in Chapter Three, the columns represent Learning Cycle Events and Integration Events. The rows are subteams, functional groups or individuals, depending upon the structure of the team. Now that you know the cadence of your learning cycles and the timing of your Integration Events, you are ready to fill in the first row of the grid. Here is the step-by-step procedure to get the row and column headers on the plan:

1. Make column headings with sticky notes—one sticky note per Learning Cycle Event or Integration Event (LC1, IE3, etc).

2. Divide the paper or whiteboard into a grid with enough columns for all of your column labels. Reserve one column on the left for row headings and three columns on the far right.

3. Put your column heading sticky notes on the top row in order. Each Integration Event will be immediately to the right of the last learning cycle that precedes it.

4. Add three more columns to the far right of the report: Closed, Not Closed and Later.

5. Decide how to use the rows in the plan, and make sticky notes for the row headers. This makes them easier to rearrange until they are in a natural order that makes sense to the team.

Now that you have the row and column headers, it's time to populate the plan.

The Final Learning Cycles Plan

You are ready to build the Learning Cycles Plan. Break your team into subgroups based on the row headings you have determined. For a small team, you may have people work individually.

Place Key Decisions

First, take a moment to write a second set of sticky notes for the Key Decisions so that you can leave the team's Key Decisions Flow in place. If the team splits up the work, it takes just a few minutes. This makes it easier for the Program Leader to create an integrated Key Decisions Plan after the meeting.

Then ask each subgroup to move the duplicate Key Decisions onto the Learning Cycles Plan, placing them in the appropriate Integration Event columns. When the team finishes, all of its Key Decisions will be in two places: on the Key Decisions Flow and on the Learning Cycles Plan, which will have only Key Decisions on it.

It is possible for a few Key Decisions to be made between Integration Events, if they can be made within the team without consulting many people. If you have any of these, put them in the learning cycle where the decision will be made.

Validate the Key Decision Flow

Now get the entire team in front of the Learning Cycles Plan. Start at the end of the program and walk backward through the plan to validate that Key Decisions are in the right places. This step of the process exposes any misalignments across subteams, and usually leads to a rich discussion about the sequence of events.

You may find that you need to add or remove Integration Events at this point. It's easier to make these changes now, before the Knowledge Gaps are on the board. If you end up with any Integration Events that lack Key Decisions, you may remove them as long as doing so does not create a gap of more than twelve weeks between Integration Events.

You may find that one subteam is expecting another subteam to make a decision much earlier than it plans to make the decision. Teams can add provisional decisions that they finalize later or can break a Key Decision down into smaller decisions so that one subteam is not waiting on another subteam to move forward. Procurement and other downstream partners can find ways to work with sets of alternatives or partial information so that the final Key Decision can be made at the Last Responsible Moment.

The discussion around this step is so worthwhile that we tend to let it run as long as it takes to get the team aligned on the flow of Key Decisions through Integration Events. If we get this right, the rest of the planning process goes fast.

Populate the Plan with Knowledge Gaps

Next, ask each subgroup to move the Knowledge Gaps into the plan. Each Knowledge Gap needs to be placed on the Learning Cycles Plan where it needs to start, and it should finish before the Key Decision that depends on it.

We place them in strict category order:

1. Do Now
2. Do Next
3. Prioritize
4. Do If Time

The "Do Not Close" items can go directly into a "Do Not Close" column at the end of the plan. But the team may also need to place other items in that column. We often have "Do If Time" Knowledge Gaps that cannot be placed on the Learning Cycles Plan in time for their Key Decisions without taking high criticality Knowledge Gaps off the plan. We also put these into the "Do Not Close" column immediately.

It's OK to rearrange high criticality Knowledge Gaps to optimize the plan, but the team needs to be careful not to overload the plan. The Program Leader can help by checking to make sure that Knowledge Gaps with long durations get more than one learning cycle, and that no learning cycle contains more than one medium to long Knowledge Gap for each subteam unless they know that they'll have waiting time that they can use.

When this step is finished, each Knowledge Gap will be assigned to a learning cycle or placed in the "Do Not Close" column.

Add Dates to the Plan

Using the team's cadence, assign the end date of every learning cycle. If your cycle is three weeks long and ends on a Friday, the first learning cycle will end on the third Friday after the Kickoff Event, and then another learning cycle will end every third Friday after that.

The end date is the date of your Learning Cycle Event, so you may need to agree now on the day of the week for that event, which is the same day of the week on which you will hold Integration Events.

Write these end dates on your column header sticky notes. The date of an Integration Event is the same date as the end of the learning cycle immediately to the left of the Integration Event.

This is the point at which the Learning Cycles Plan goes from abstraction to reality. It's a good time to have a sanity check with the team: Does the plan reflect what they commit to do? Is any work going on that's not on this plan but should be? Is there any work they are doing right now on the program that should stop based on this plan? What will get in the way of executing the plan for the first learning cycle?

By the time you have completed this process, each person on the team should know what Knowledge Gap he or she is working on, starting tomorrow morning. Team members may start asking at this point, "OK, I get that I'm supposed to close this Knowledge Gap, but what am I supposed to DO?" They may ask for a Gantt chart or a detailed deliverables list. These are signs that people are worried about activities.

Where Are the Activities and Deliverables?

We don't convert the Learning Cycles Plan to an Activity Plan at the team level. That is done by the individuals or subteams responsible for closing Knowledge Gaps. You as the Program Leader can work with your subteam leaders to help them build Activity Plans, and you can ask that these Activity Plans be shared with you, but it's not helpful for the team as a whole to spend any time on them. At the team level, we keep all our attention on learning. The team's focus should be on closing Knowledge Gaps to make better Key Decisions.

I don't mean to say that activities and deliverables are not important. Requirements definitions, technical specifications and similar documents, even renderings and CAD models, capture all of the decisions that the team has made about the product design—not just the Key Decisions that drive the product's success. These decisions need to be communicated to suppliers, manufacturing engineers, technical writers and other partners. Most traditional PDP standards include checklists to ensure that none of these key deliverables get missed.

Yet we don't put these checklist deliverables on the Learning Cycles Plan, because these documents don't capture knowledge. Instead, they capture decisions that may or may not have required the team to build knowledge, without a place to include any new knowledge the team has created.

The traditional PDP doesn't recognize the value of the knowledge behind the program's most important decisions, has no place to put such knowledge, and allows for no time to capture it.

For most of the thousands of low impact or well-understood decisions that get made within a product development program, this is acceptable, if not ideal. These low-level decisions are likely to be right the first time, and if they do need to be changed, that is relatively easy to do.

For such decisions, there is little knowledge to build or to capture. We acknowledge this by keeping such deliverables off the Learning Cycles Plan where they won't distract the team from its core mission to build the knowledge needed to make Key Decisions.

The First Update to the Learning Cycles Plan

As soon as people leave the room, they realize that there are things that are not covered by the plan as it stands. They will recognize that some of the work they've already done, or that they have in progress, is not reflected in the plan. Sometimes this means they have been working on the wrong things and should be redirected. Sometimes the team has missed a Knowledge Gap or a Key Decision and the plan needs to be updated.

They will also think of missing Knowledge Gaps in the shower, when they check their email or on the drive to work in the morning. These are all good candidates for Knowledge Gaps, but they haven't received the same level of attention as the ones that arose during the Kickoff Event. You need to capture them and integrate them into the plan.

The day after the Kickoff Event, send an email to the team to ask them to make sticky notes for any new Knowledge Gaps or Key Decisions, and to put them someplace where you will find them—on your desk or on a whiteboard. Anyone who submits a new Key Decision needs to break it down into its Knowledge Gaps. The submitters should go ahead and rate the Knowledge Gaps.

The first Status Event will need extra time, because this is when you will add these new items to the plan. Just as you did during the Kickoff Event, assign owners to the new items, and ask them to incorporate the items into the plan. Typically, they will add them to a learning cycle.

They can also choose to put them in the Not Closed column, as before. They may need to renegotiate the priority of other items, if the new ones throw a subteam into overload. If there are a lot of new items, especially for a single row, you can meet with the subteam in that row before the Status Event, and then the subteam can present the new plan to the whole team.

Regular Updates to the Learning Cycles Plan

After the Learning Cycles Plan has a few days to settle, it normally gets a minor update at each Learning Cycle Event and a major update at an Integration Event. A minor update consists of giving the row owners a few minutes to make adjustments and then tell the rest of the team what they have done. A major update works like a mini Kickoff Event: review the Key Decisions, focusing on the ones for the next three Integration Events, then review the Knowledge Gaps related to those decisions.

You may need to watch out for the "snowplow" effect: Knowledge Gaps that don't close on time get pushed into the next learning cycle, causing the team to get overloaded. The first column of the Learning Cycles Plan is covered with Knowledge Gaps that have been delayed. To mitigate and prevent this, keep two things in mind:

- **Learning cycles are timeboxes.** The Knowledge Gap owners don't get more time, unless they have a good reason. The point is to learn as much as possible in the time that has been allocated, and then make a recommendation. Our goal is to reduce uncertainty—not eliminate it entirely. If the Key Decision related to the Knowledge Gap is at the Last Responsible Moment, the team has no more time and should move on to something else, or the whole team will need to accept a schedule slip.

- **If the recommendation is to "learn more," something else has to get pushed down the priority list, and that probably means it gets taken off the plan.** That may be the right decision, but it should be a team decision, not a decision made in isolation by an overloaded team member.

The next chapter describes the events that will help guide the team as it closes these Knowledge Gaps.

CHAPTER NINE

Rapid Learning Cycle Events

The shift from doing to learning is hard for most of us. We are comfortable reporting on what we have done and speculating on what we plan to do. It's not easy to talk about what we have learned and what we still need to learn, especially if we are being asked to make interpretations or recommendations that we would not have made in the past.

For experienced product developers, most team events have consisted of status updates centered around the project plan: how well is the team conforming to the plan, what's coming up next on the plan and what issues are in the way of the plan. The plan tells them what to do, how long it should take and when to do it. Sometimes, the plan is the team's plan and sometimes it's only the project manager's plan. In most traditional product development teams, it is an Activity Plan centered on producing deliverables and completing checklist items. It's assumed to be a stable plan that should not change very often if the project was well planned.

The Learning Cycles Plan is centered around learning, not activities. It contains Key Decisions and Knowledge Gaps, not deliverables and milestones. It reflects the team's best current understanding of the most important Knowledge Gaps and Key Decisions, and we expect it to change often as the team builds knowledge, makes decisions and converges on solutions. The focus of the Rapid Learning Cycles framework is on making good Key Decisions by building the body of knowledge the team needs to make those decisions: learning vs. doing.

In this chapter, I'll review the events that maintain this shift, and then describe how to integrate them with the phases and gates of a traditional PDP.

Events Maintain the Doing-to-Learning Shift

The purpose of the events is to maintain the shift from doing to learning in the following ways:

- **Provide a time and place for status updates that is fast and frequent.** The team does need to stay coordinated on its activities and deliverables, even in early development. A daily or weekly standup meeting fills the need to surface activity-level issues quickly with minimal impact on the team.

- **Plan activities after Knowledge Gaps at a separate event at the individual or subteam level.** The time to create the Activity Plan is after the Learning Cycles Plan has been created or updated, not on the same day at the same time. Usually, teams need a day or so to reflect on the Learning Cycles Plan before defining the specific activities to close Knowledge Gaps. Creating the Activity Plan later also maintains the separation between learning and doing.

- **Maintain strict separation of boundaries between status reporting, knowledge sharing and decision making.** Do whatever you need to do to keep status reports out of your Learning Cycle Events. Teams can hold Status Events before their Learning Cycle Events. If you try this, consider taking a break outside the room before starting the Learning Cycle Event. Team members can review each other's Knowledge Gap Reports to ensure that the focus is kept on what was learned vs. what was done.

- **Ensure that the team's new knowledge gets recorded in every cycle.** A Key Decision is not complete until the rationale for that decision has been documented, and a Knowledge Gap has not been closed until the knowledge has been captured. This does not have to be complicated: simple, single-sided reports work well.

- **Hold people accountable for sharing interpretations and recommendations—not just activities and data.** It's hard to explain the rationale for a recommendation or a decision if you're not allowed to share what you did to learn what you learned. But if a team member describes an experiment and reports the data without offering an interpretation and a recommendation, ask for them. Without this analysis, the team hasn't learned anything. This is especially important when working with new engineers. Since they lack experience, they may hesitate to offer their opinions. But they will learn much faster if they do give interpretations and then listen to the feedback.

- **Stop doing anything that does not contribute to Learning.** If you are closing a Knowledge Gap and you encounter an activity that will not generate useful knowledge, call a time-out. Talk to the Program Leader or your engineering team lead about what you observe and what you recommend instead. If you have an idea for a different approach that will generate the same knowledge but faster, better or cheaper, that's what you should do instead. Well-formulated Knowledge Gap questions make it easier to recognize when there is a mismatch between an activity and its related Knowledge Gap.

The Kickoff Event

A Kickoff Event is essential for the success of the Rapid Learning Cycles framework. Everyone on the team needs to understand how you have adapted the Rapid Learning Cycles framework and the Key Decisions and

Knowledge Gaps they are responsible for. There is no written document you can create that takes the place of the discussion that goes into the plan. It would take weeks to try to communicate the results without getting everyone in the same room. Teams that attempt to use the framework without this step have expended a lot of wasted energy struggling to get coordinated. If you try to set up a Rapid Learning Cycles framework without a Kickoff Event, don't be surprised when it all falls apart within a quarter.

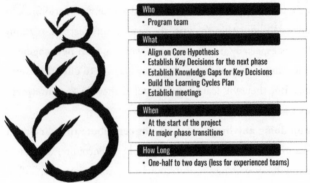

Who
• Program team

What
• Align on Core Hypothesis
• Establish Key Decisions for the next phase
• Establish Knowledge Gaps for Key Decisions
• Build the Learning Cycles Plan
• Establish meetings

When
• At the start of the project
• At major phase transitions

How Long
• One-half to two days (less for experienced teams)

Figure 9.1: The Kickoff Event

One or Two Focused Days

We structure a Kickoff Event as a half- to two-day event for the whole team, ideally held away from the office. A collocated team that has used the framework before will be able to get through a Kickoff Event in half a day. The first one takes longer because you need to explain and provide coaching to the team at every step.

The team has some very important things to get done at this meeting—the work described in Chapters Four and Five to build the Learning Cycles Plan.

1. Review the Core Hypothesis and high-level schedule for the project.

2. Determine the first-pass list of Key Decisions that the team needs to make.

3. Determine the initial set of Knowledge Gaps.

4. Establish cadences for team events.

5. Define the Learning Cycles Plan.

We have a lot of resources and templates at the Rapid Learning Cycles Resource Center (see Appendix D) to help you set up this meeting. They all assume that the entire team is in the room with you. But if you want to run this meeting virtually, this framework won't help you.

Face to Face

A lot of flexibility is built into the Rapid Learning Cycles framework, but this is not one of those flexible places. If you are prepared to invest thousands or millions of dollars in development, you should be willing to spend a few thousand more to get the team together in one place to clarify the product's Core Hypothesis and define the Learning Cycles Plan.

The team will use paper charts, whiteboards and sticky notes in this meeting, the easiest tools for visual collaboration, requiring no technology more advanced than a permanent marker. The plan gets developed through a participative process that builds working relationships, surfaces conflicts when they are easiest to resolve and helps the team internalize the structure of the product and the team framework. Communication is much better after the individuals have gone back home, and the relationships endure for the length of the project.

While I was still at Hewlett Packard, a long-planned face-to-face kickoff for a global project was canceled due to an end-of-fiscal-year travel freeze, a corporate-wide last-ditch effort to cut expenses before the final numbers came in. We attempted to hold a "kickoff" as a series of web conferences, but people didn't know each other well and had divergent views of the project's goals.

There was a lot of conflict that is obvious in hindsight but at the same time was entirely hidden because we were not in the same room. This remote "kickoff" left us with a muddled, confusing charter that reflected the team's misalignment. The project never recovered, and three teams spent two years working against each other. By the time the program manager was able to bring the teams together to resolve the conflicts, it was too late to save the project. To this day, I am convinced that if we had only been able to resolve our differences from the beginning, through building relationships and developing a strong charter as a team, we could have delivered a great product. Instead, to save less than $20,000 in travel costs, the company wasted more than $10 million in development costs.

Despite this experience, I have attempted to run Kickoff Events remotely, using some of the best videoconferencing systems out there. But the fact remains that the people who are not in the main room with the Program Leader are largely shut out of the process, no matter what we do. At events like this, the best ideas often emerge during morning coffee, lunches and breaks. A lot of informal lobbying takes place at the espresso machine, leaving the person on the video screen shut out of the places where the real decisions get made.

After watching teams struggle again and again, I will no longer make the effort. If you believe in the product, and in the people who will help you build it, and if you want to see it come to life as quickly as possible, this one face-to-face meeting is worth every penny you spend on it, and every night away from home.

A Plan with Momentum

After this meeting, you will have a Learning Cycles Plan with Knowledge Gaps and Key Decisions. Your next step will be to enter the Key Decisions and Knowledge Gaps into their logs. It's best to let no more than twenty-four hours go by before doing this. A major failure mode occurs when the documentation from the Kickoff Event does not get produced quickly enough afterward. You also need to put the Learning Cycles Plan where people can see it. If it has to be available online, it needs to be online as quickly as possible after the meeting.

A couple of years ago, I worked with a team that had launched Rapid Learning Cycles on their own and then called me when they ran into trouble. One major problem was that the program manager, who was exceptionally busy, had created a complicated Virtual Visual Plan that only he could update. It was never updated during the meeting itself—and it took him days to get it updated.

On a complex project, it's so easy for people to walk away from a meeting with a different understanding of the agreements that have been made. In this case, without a reference, people got off track quickly. This misalignment burned up a lot of time that the team didn't have. We fixed the problem by simplifying the plan, and by establishing twenty-four-hour turnaround for online updates to the plan. The program manager made that his first priority after leaving the meeting. With that new rule in place, the team was able to make much faster progress.

When your team members get back to the office, they will know exactly what they need to start learning. You will be ready to lead your first Status Event.

The Status Event

In the Rapid Learning Cycles framework, we spend the least amount of time on status reporting that we need to surface problems. The best way to do that is to adapt the standup meeting from Agile Software Development: fifteen-minute daily meetings held without chairs, where only three questions get asked and only two answers are acceptable.

It may sound silly, but it is important to run these meetings with everyone standing who is able. This is not a meeting for settling down with a cup of coffee. It should be an energizing gathering of the team's forces before going out to conquer the Knowledge Gaps in front of you. Standing up helps build that momentum.

Your team will probably be just a little uncomfortable, which will encourage them to end the meeting quickly. The lack of chairs gives people freedom to move around a bit more, to move closer to a colleague who has an issue that they can help with. We also help the team focus with a tight agenda that should last no more than fifteen to thirty minutes.

A Simple Structure

The structure of the meeting is simple: each person gets a minute or so to answer three questions: "What have I done? What will I do? What's in my way?" The only allowable responses from anyone are "Thank you" and "I can help with that." Everything else stays out of the meeting: troubleshooting, problem solving, even planning the time for a follow-up meeting. All those discussions happen outside the room between the individual and those who can help.

This is a difficult discipline to establish. It goes against our conditioning about what happens in meetings. Yet it is the most effective way to surface problems without taking much of the team's time. You as the Program Leader will need to be heavy-handed at first to shut down discussions that take these meetings off track. You will need to monitor your own behavior carefully. After a few successful Status Events, the team will be able to police itself.

Often, But Not Too Often

We find that a daily Status Event is usually too often for a team using the Rapid Learning Cycles framework. Weekly or twice-weekly meetings work well for many teams. Some teams with long learning cycles have them every two weeks, and find that is enough.

The entire team participates in Status Events, but they can be structured in different ways. The entire team can hold one Status Event, or subteams can hold their own. The team can meet in front of the Learning Cycles Plan or in front of an Activity Plan. You as the Program Leader will attend every one of the Status Events at first. This will require some coordination.

Status Events can be held virtually, but it's better to hold them within subteams that are collocated as much as possible. They are so short that any technology issue is going to prevent remote participants from getting any value. It's not worth the overhead to set up a video link—at least not until it's as easy to set up a videoconference as it is to walk into a room. You will need to take special care with remote teams to make sure that they surface problems to you, since you cannot be there in person.

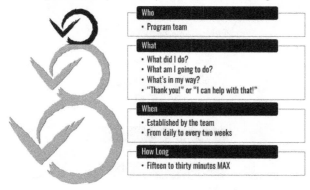

Who
- Program team

What
- What did I do?
- What am I going to do?
- What's in my way?
- "Thank you!" or "I can help with that!"

When
- Established by the team
- From daily to every two weeks

How Long
- Fifteen to thirty minutes MAX

Figure 9.2: The Status Event

In your Kickoff Event, you will have defined the timing and frequency for your Status Events. You probably have one coming up quickly. Even if the Kickoff Event was on Friday and you agreed to do Status Events every Monday, you need to have the first Status Event on Monday. No one will have anything to report, but there will probably be some changes to the Learning Cycles Plan. At this first meeting only, it is OK to take some extra time to incorporate these changes. After the first meeting, you will adjust the Learning Cycles Plan between Learning Cycle Events only if something major happens.

The Learning Cycle Event

A Learning Cycle Event happens at the boundary between the end of one learning cycle and the start of the next one. The purpose of this event is to share the knowledge that the team has built to close its Knowledge Gaps. Every Knowledge Gap owner with an active Knowledge Gap gives a short report on what he or she has learned, with recommendations for what to do next. The audience is the entire team.

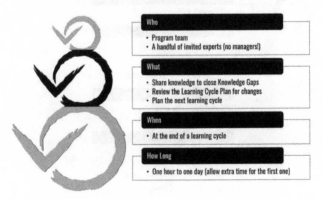

Who
- Program team
- A handful of invited experts (no managers!)

What
- Share knowledge to close Knowledge Gaps
- Review the Learning Cycle Plan for changes
- Plan the next learning cycle

When
- At the end of a learning cycle

How Long
- One hour to one day (allow extra time for the first one)

Figure 9.3: The Learning Cycle Event

Only the People You Need

This meeting is for the team, and the format for the meeting varies widely from group to group. Some large teams split up Learning Cycle Events among subteams so that software engineers, for example, don't have to listen to metallurgical details that have no relevance for them. Other large teams require the subteam leaders to attend, with open invitations to anyone else on the team who wants to join. If the team is small enough, everyone attends.

But extra people don't attend unless they are invited for a specific reason. This is not a management review meeting, not an executive status update and not a forum for partners who have not been engaged with the program team to give feedback. It's not helpful to the team at this point to have a lot of outsiders asking questions that have already been answered in other ways. It's especially not helpful to have managers there who do not understand the Rapid Learning Cycles framework, and therefore expect the team to be doing rather than learning.

Learning Cycle Events work well remotely, as long as the group takes frequent breaks and the audio and video quality are good. If the remote participants can see and hear the Knowledge Gap owners who are in the room, and if the participants in the room can see and hear the remote Knowledge Gap owners as they present, then knowledge sharing works just fine remotely.

Just a Little Preparation

To prepare for the Learning Cycle Event, Knowledge Gap owners write short reports that outline the knowledge they have gained. Some groups like using a simple, standardized slide—one for each Knowledge Gap, with at most three backup slides. Other groups like using A3 reports (reports on one single side of A3 or Tabloid paper). In all cases, you as the Program Leader will establish a template for these reports so that all Knowledge Gap owners present their knowledge and recommendations in the same way. This helps keep the reports concise.

Here are the recommendations that Knowledge Gap owners can make:

- **Close the Knowledge Gap.** Knowledge Gap owners can recommend that the Knowledge Gap be closed because the knowledge is now available to the team.

- **Move the Knowledge Gap to the Not Closed column.** They can recommend that the Knowledge Gap be moved to the Not Closed column if problems have cropped up that will make it difficult to close, or if the team is out of time to close it.

- **Keep working on the Knowledge Gap.** The Knowledge Gap owners can recommend that they continue their experiments to close the Knowledge Gap, if its Key Decision is not yet at the Last Responsible Moment. This may be a common recommendation, especially at first. The whole team must consider this within the context of the entire program, including the impact on the other Knowledge Gaps. If this work continues, something else will need to be delayed or removed.

If a Knowledge Gap extends across learning cycles, there is no need for the Knowledge Gap owner to present a report, unless something has changed that requires the team's input.

A Simple Agenda

Learning Cycle Events normally take at least two hours and up to an entire day if there are a lot of Knowledge Gaps to cover. A typical agenda for a Learning Cycle Event looks like this:

- Status Event followed by a break

- Review of any major changes to the program from the Program Leader—new people, changes to the Core Hypothesis
- Knowledge Gap Reports
- Review of the Learning Cycles Plan with updates
- Agreement on the Knowledge Gaps that will be active in the next learning cycle

As the Program Leader, you will need to make sure there is enough time at the end to review the plan and make agreements. Otherwise, the team will enter the next learning cycle in a state of misalignment about what to do next. The event doesn't end until everyone knows exactly what they will start working on tomorrow.

The Integration Event

Integration Events happen at the Last Responsible Moment for making groups of Key Decisions. When building the Learning Cycles Plan, your team defined the actual Last Responsible Moments when Key Decisions needed to be made. They then adjusted the Last Responsible Moments so that the Key Decisions fit into Integration Events that take place at the end of learning cycles.

Unlike the learning cycles themselves, Integration Events can occur irregularly. Your team can vary the number of learning cycles between Integration Events without getting out of step. However, it does cause disruption for the team if you do an Integration Event in the middle of a learning cycle.

The Right People in the Room

The purpose of an Integration Event is to make Key Decisions. To facilitate that, we gather everyone who needs to be involved in making these decisions into the same room at the same time. This builds the alignment you need so that these major decisions stick. The invitation list is usually broader than just the team, and varies from event to event based upon the specific decisions that need to be made. You may need to invite functional partners, program sponsors and perhaps even key customers, investors or vendors to some of the events.

To keep the meeting on track, you will need to brief these "extra" participants ahead of time, ideally in a one-on-one meeting. This briefing focuses on the knowledge your team has developed for the Key Decisions that they will be asked to make. This gives the decision makers a chance to digest this knowledge and ask questions about it ahead of the Integration Event, so that the event itself can focus on the decision to be made.

Simple, Focused Reports with Recommendations

Each Key Decision needs a short summary of the current state of the knowledge the team has developed, and a recommended decision from the team. Normally, the Key Decision owner or the Program Leader prepares this summary. The Program Leader distributes these Key Decision Reports to the decision makers in advance of the event, along with the related Knowledge Gap Reports.

You can adapt the Key Decision Report format from the team's format for Knowledge Gap Reports. That makes it easier for the team to write them and for others to read them as a package. Again, do not bog down the meeting with extensive slide sets—even if this is the way that your stakeholders and leaders expect you to communicate.

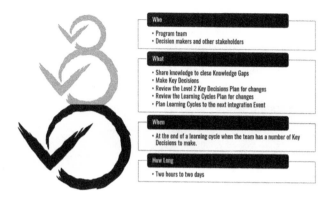

Who
- Program team
- Decision makers and other stakeholders

What
- Share knowledge to close Knowledge Gaps
- Make Key Decisions
- Review the Level 2 Key Decisions Plan for changes
- Review the Learning Cycles Plan for changes
- Plan Learning Cycles to the next Integration Event

When
- At the end of a learning cycle when the team has a number of Key Decisions to make.

How Long
- Two hours to two days

Figure 9.4: The Integration Event

This is one time to break that rule so that you get a good, well-informed discussion that leads to good decisions. If your participants are like the leaders I've worked with, they will be uncomfortable for no more than two meetings. Then they will find themselves feeling relieved that your meetings are more interesting and engaging and lead to better outcomes.

The person writing the Key Decision report should make a clear recommendation:

- A decision to take a specific course of action.
- A provisional decision that accounts for knowledge the team has not yet been able to get, without delaying the product.
- A decision to take more time to learn, and therefore delay the product.

Most of the time, even if the Knowledge Gaps have not been perfectly closed, the team has built enough new knowledge to make a decision. If that is not the case, the next best option is to make a "best guess" decision and track the unclosed Knowledge Gaps as risks. This is not that different from the way the team would have behaved in the past—except that they know the risk they are taking. Only in extreme circumstances do you want to delay the program.

Some isolated Key Decisions that affect only one or a few subsystems may be made prior to the meeting and reported during the next Integration Event. Major decisions that affect the entire team should be handled within the Integration Event.

An Event "Sandwich"

The Integration Event is a sandwich: it begins with the first part of a Learning Cycle Event, moves to Key Decisions and then goes back to the second part of the Learning Cycle Event. It's helpful to have your decision makers and stakeholders participate in the first part, but encourage them to leave before the team starts the second part of the Learning Cycle Event, which is where the planning takes place.

Here is a sample agenda:

- Status Event followed by a break
- Review of any major changes to the program from the Program Leader—new people, changes to the Core Hypothesis
- Knowledge Gap and Key Decision Reports—this is where Key Decisions get made
- Break to allow stakeholders and partners to leave
- Review of the Learning Cycles Plan with updates
- Agreement on the Key Decisions to be addressed in the next three Integration Events
- Updating of the Learning Cycles Plan for the Knowledge Gaps to be investigated in the learning cycles that lead up to the next Integration Event
- Agreement on the Knowledge Gaps that will be active in the next learning cycle

These events take longer than Learning Cycle Events—up to twice as long. If there are a lot of new people who will ask a lot of questions, or if there are a lot of Key Decisions to discuss, you will need a lot of extra time. The Learning Cycles Plan update will also take longer because you will be looking at Key Decisions as well as Knowledge Gaps, and there will probably be changes based on the outcome of the meeting.

The Rapid Learning Cycles Framework in a Phase Gate Lifecycle

If you work in a corporate R&D environment, chances are you have a Product Development Process (PDP) with phases/stages and gates. The Rapid Learning Cycles framework integrates well with this top-level program structure. But the details of the PDP, especially in early development, usually need adaptation.

If you are piloting the Rapid Learning Cycles framework, get permission before you start to break the rules. Eliminate deliverables and other checklist items that don't contribute to the group's ability to close Knowledge Gaps. Move others, such as technical specifications, to the Last Responsible Moment, which is usually a lot later than these documents are typically due. Eliminate large "data dumps" on downstream partners and work with them more concurrently by incorporating them into your learning cycles, where they can work with your team on closing one Knowledge Gap at a time.

Your biggest challenge will be those groups downstream of you who are used to working in silos. Testing groups, process development groups and procurement organizations often believe that it is more efficient for them to wait until the product design is "frozen" before they start their work. This may be true for them, but it is not true for the PDP as a whole.

Such beliefs lengthen the distance between you and your finished product. Push back on these beliefs with everything you have. Work with your downstream partners to understand what they need to take their first steps vs. what they would like to have. We all would like a product design that is flawless, but if it's being designed without input from Testing, Process Development, Manufacturing or Procurement, they will find issues with it when it finally reaches them.

The phases and gates themselves are not a problem. In fact, the stages provide a way to focus the team on the most important Key Decisions. In Concept Evaluation, the Key Decision is: "go/no-go." In Feasibility, the Key Decisions relate to customer needs, value propositions, core technology choices and the markets that will be pursued. As the program moves into Detailed Design, the Key Decisions and Knowledge Gaps focus more on eliminating the outstanding technical and customer interface risks that could derail the program.

If the phase gate process is well designed, each gate represents an additional level of investment in the product. This often means that additional team members or new functional groups get engaged. It may be helpful to hold additional Kickoff Events at these major transitions to bring the new people on board, and to ensure that the team's plan reflects the new state of the program.

The gates provide natural points for the team to stop and reflect on where they are and where they need to go. It's a chance for the team to get feedback from product development leaders who may be unable to attend Integration Events. It's not a good idea to combine a Gate Review with an Integration Event. That only encourages the senior leaders to involve themselves in implementation issues, rather than assessing the program's strategic fit and business case.

Instead, I would hold the Integration Event a few days before the Gate Review, and then feed the outcome into the Gate Review. The Gate Review should be a management control point for discussing the health of the business case for the product and its strategic fit within the overall product development portfolio.

The Rapid Learning Cycles framework tends to surface the types of intractable problems that doom a product in the market much sooner than a traditional PDP does. More of them get killed in the early phases, and this is a good thing for the company and the team.

If a Gate Review leads to the conclusion that the project should be canceled, the team should see that as a "win"—by learning what they have learned and making that visible to management as soon as possible, they have saved the company a lot of time and money. They have freed themselves up to work on a product that could have much more potential value. No one wants to spend three years of their lives on a product that customers don't want to buy.

When a program makes it all the way to the start of Detailed Design, the team is ready for action. When the program transitions out of Early Development, the framework remains in place, but the team's focus changes.

The Rapid Learning Cycles Framework and the Transition out of Early Development

When the program passes through the gate that leads out of Early Development, a number of things usually happen at once:

- The organization commits the resources and money necessary to take the program to Launch. It's rare for programs to be canceled after this gate, even in a well-functioning phase gate process.

- New team members come on board. The technical team adds additional engineers, the marketing team expands and partners take a more active role.

- The final launch date gets established, with high confidence that the team will meet it.

At this phase transition, the team's focus naturally changes from learning to doing. But the need to keep learning doesn't stop. All of the unclosed Knowledge Gaps are now risks, and the team will continue to run learning cycles on the most important ones. The team continues with the Rapid Learning Cycles framework, with adjustments to accommodate this shift.

The Learning Cycles Plan continues but now runs alongside plans to track deliverables. You could use a Gantt chart for the Key Decisions, if it's helpful and the project plan is stable enough. The major deliverables can go on this plan, and the Gantt chart model will show the dependencies between them.

I still coach my clients to use visual planning for the detailed deliverables and the activities to produce them. It's best if the team continues to use the "rolling window" concept to plan out only one learning cycle's worth of activities and detailed deliverables at a time. At this level of the program, things are still likely to change a great deal.

Learning cycles continue to focus on the remaining Key Decisions and Knowledge Gaps. The team still has Key Decisions coming up, with Knowledge Gaps to close. It may run targeted learning cycles to reduce risks where it made provisional decisions because Knowledge Gaps were not closed in time. Sometimes, teams will prioritize risks and focus their learning cycles on the most important ones.

The event structure remains in place. Learning Cycle Events begin to look more like Design Reviews, and Integration Events often take the form of system prototype reviews. As deliverables close and validation tests find errors, Status Events focus less on planned activities and more on coordinating the work to fix problems. With the learning done earlier in the program, these problems tend to be less severe than they would be if the team had followed a traditional process. The team has more knowledge to use as it devises solutions.

The cadence may lengthen. It may make sense to focus Learning Cycle Events based on planned design releases to downstream partners, which may be one to two months apart, and Integration Events around prototype builds that may be several months apart. Status Events often go the other way. As the team dives deeply into the details of the design, it may decide to hold a Status Event every day to ensure that problems get dealt with immediately.

In Part Three, I'll describe the work that takes place inside the learning cycles to close Knowledge Gaps, and the role of the Program Leader in between events.

PART THREE

Inside the Learning Cycle

CHAPTER TEN

Building and Capturing Knowledge

The Learning Cycles Plan is in place, and the team is all set to go. What does it do next? Close Knowledge Gaps.

That seems obvious enough, but I've learned that just running off to get a bunch of data doesn't necessarily lead to a closed Knowledge Gap. Just as the whole program benefits from understanding what the team needs to learn before doing anything, the Knowledge Gap owner benefits from taking a little time to understand the Knowledge Gap and develop a good plan to close it.

The Goal Is a Closed Knowledge Gap

A Knowledge Gap is closed when you have the information you need to feed into the Key Decision. That doesn't mean you know everything there is to know. But you have done enough investigation to feel confident in your recommendations, and the decision won't have to be revisited later.

Innovators usually know when a Knowledge Gap has been closed well enough. At the same time, this intuition is more or less trustworthy. If the topic is entirely new to you, the market is new, or the customer or technology is new, then your internal instincts are more likely to be wrong.

Depending on your personality, this uncertainty can paralyze you or lead you to take imprudent risks.

For that reason, it's helpful to set up an external standard for the amount of evidence you need to support your recommendation. This is especially important if you are working with a small team and little outside accountability. Get comfortable asking each other the question, "What evidence do you see to support this?" This will help guard against the confirmation bias that tends to make our predictions overly optimistic.

You set your own standards most of the time. If you are comfortable taking more risk, the evidence barrier can be lower. Aerospace companies require a lot of evidence, in the form of simulation models, engineering calculations with lots of margin for error and physical testing, before they'll put a test pilot's life on the line. Pharma companies have strict protocols for the products that reach First Human Dose. People in these industries maintain high standards of evidence, and they willingly pay the price in terms of speed and cost.

But what if you are developing a new iPad app? You know that Apple will test the app for any destructive behavior, and will give you a strict sandbox to play in. One set of Knowledge Gaps may relate to the need to pass Apple's tests. But you also know that the product can be updated frequently as you make improvements, and that iPad owners like to see actively developed apps that evolve to become better and better.

The biggest risk you have is that someone else will beat you to market or that you will be ignored in the App Store. Worst case, the app bombs or nobody cares. You are mainly out your own time, and you can just try again. In this case, your standards of evidence will be lower because the overall program risk is lower. But you probably still have Key Decisions to make and Knowledge Gaps to close.

The Scientific Method Closes Knowledge Gaps

If you have an engineering or scientific background, you already know how to close Knowledge Gaps. It is nothing more than the Scientific Method that has been practiced since the 1700s. In my elementary school, I learned it in fourth grade.

Figure 1.2: The Scientific Method

The method, as shown in Figure 10.1 may seem procedural—a far cry from the freewheeling atmosphere that supposedly fosters creativity in innovation teams and startups. But that's true only if you define "creativity" as unpredictable chaos. You need creativity to generate the hypotheses from your observations and develop new methods of validating the ideas. The Scientific Method provides a mechanism to prove your ideas so that you can say, with confidence, that your hypothesis is correct—that you have closed the Knowledge Gap.

In practice, the Scientific Method can be a bit unwieldy for product development, because it was designed for academic research. There are a number of other methods that adapt the Scientific Method to situations that demand less rigor.

It doesn't matter which method you choose to close Knowledge Gaps, so long as your team has one. It should be robust enough to ensure that the team does not redo work that others have already done, the experimental design is built around the hypothesis and the knowledge gets written down and shared. It should be lightweight enough to use on a simple Knowledge Gap that you can close with a few hours of research or lab work.

Build–Test–Fix and Build–Measure–Learn Are Not Enough

The Scientific Method is not Build–Test–Fix, and it is more robust than Build–Measure–Learn. Both of these begin with the "build" step—but how do you know that the thing you are building is the right thing to help you learn? How do you know that building anything is the best way to learn what you most need to learn right now? A product build is one type of model, but there are many other models and experimental designs to choose from. Some of these are a lot faster and more conclusive.

In science, giant hypotheses get broken down into smaller hypotheses that can be tested much faster. If someone wants to study the effects of serotonin levels on longevity, that's hard to study in humans or even other primates. But in animals with shorter natural lifespans, we can see the effects and then speculate (but not confirm) whether or not that effect is also present in humans.

We might find ways to conduct noninvasive human experiments that get around the longevity issue, such as studying serotonin in the elderly and performing studies on the brains of subjects who died at different ages. Eventually, a consensus may emerge that the scientific community has confidence in, even though the invasive longitudinal studies we need to confirm the consensus are too difficult to perform.

In product development, we do the same thing: Build–Test–Fix is basically one giant experiment to validate the Core Hypothesis, with all the activity going into running this big experiment. But we know a lot about how to break that Core Hypothesis down into smaller pieces that we can test independently with observational studies, modeling, experimentation and, finally, beta testing with real customers.

We learn everything we can at less expense before we start building full system prototypes. Build–Measure–Learn is a slight improvement over Build–Test–Fix once you're in the Execution Phase, if you've defined the measures correctly. But I would still challenge the team to build only when that's the best way to close their most important Knowledge Gaps.

Design–Experiment–Capture

The best description of what happens inside a learning cycles boils down to three words: Design–Experiment–Capture. This reinforces the aspects of the Scientific Method that are the most important for closing Knowledge Gaps effectively and efficiently to maximize the value of learning.

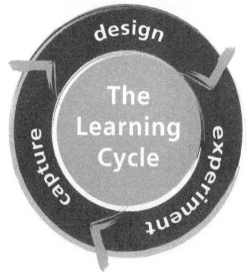

Figure 1.3: Learning Cycles of Design–Experiment–Capture

- **Design.** Take a little time to figure out the most efficient way to close the Knowledge Gap. It helps to understand the hypotheses that are embedded in the Knowledge Gap so that you can design experiments to close it.
- **Experiment.** Run the experiment and analyze the data to develop conclusions and recommendations.
- **Capture.** Write the Knowledge Gap report and any supplemental reports you want to create to capture what you have just learned for your own team and for future teams.

Every Knowledge Gap represents one or more potential hypotheses. The Knowledge Gap represented by the question "What options do we have for materials for the load-bearing part of the product?" becomes two hypotheses:

- "5,000 kg of load-bearing capacity is enough to provide structural stability for our product."
- "These five alternative materials will all support at least 5,000 kg of weight."

You can probably test the first hypothesis with engineering calculations. The second hypothesis requires some research into the specific properties of the materials. Eventually, you will need to do some physical testing, but you don't need the entire finished product to do that testing. You may be able to get away with a much simpler physical model.

Within just a few learning cycles, your team will get smart about how to test hypotheses with as little work as possible. The Rapid Learning Cycles framework imposes a timebox on learning that encourages creativity in designing experiments. When there is not time to build, the team will find alternative experimental or analytical models that work well enough to support their recommendations.

Good Models Maximize Learning

The quality of the knowledge that someone builds with a Design–Experiment–Capture cycle is entirely dependent on the quality of the experimental model. It determines the confidence you have in the results and the recommendations that proceed from it. But this does not mean that your models have to be perfect. Remember that "All models are wrong—some are useful."

We take time to formulate a good hypothesis so that we know how to test for it and when it has been confirmed. Then we look for a model to assess the hypothesis that is:

- **Fast.** What is the minimum you can do to validate this hypothesis with enough confidence to proceed? What can you do that involves the fewest number of people? What can you do that takes the least amount of time and effort? What can you do with the time you have?

- **Cheap.** What is the lowest resolution you truly need to get the data? Do you need a whole product or just a subsystem in a harness? Do you need a production-ready part, or will a 3D print work well enough? Do you need a physical model, or can you use simulation tools? Do you need a computerized model, or will a few whiteboard sketches help you think it through?

- **Conclusive.** What is "good enough" validation for this hypothesis, at this point in the program?

I get it that sometimes your hands almost itch with the desire to put something—anything—together that resembles your product vision. But I also know that you don't have all the time you need and all the money you want. The shortest distance between you and your vision sometimes goes through models that test only a small piece of that vision, to make sure that the entire product comes together before you run out of time, money and patience.

The quality of your model also determines how extensible your knowledge is to different situations: Will you have to do this work again if the parameters for the product change, even slightly? Or is the knowledge robust enough that future products can also leverage it?

Extensible Models Preserve Flexibility

Experiments that build extensible knowledge create value for future programs by turning one team's Key Decision into another team's Known Solution. Extensible knowledge also helps the current team by developing knowledge that gives the team more flexibility. If something doesn't work as expected, the team has greater understanding about how the pieces of the system interact and therefore what's easiest to change and most likely to work.

Here are a few principles about how to design a model that builds extensible knowledge:

- **Test ranges, not points.** Build–Test–Fix is all about testing single-point full-scale models until you stumble on a solution. You'll find the solution a lot faster if you test a range of alternatives around your preferred solution. You won't waste a cycle just because the point you chose was 10 percent away from the point that you needed. If your design has to work together with other components, you're giving your design partners a lot more freedom to operate. As a bonus, you generate extensible knowledge. Another team working on a similar product (or perhaps your team working on the next product) probably has similar trade-offs to consider. You've just created a lot of knowledge to evaluate these trade-offs for a product that has slightly different parameters.

- **Test to failure.** Find the place where your hypothesis breaks down. When testing weight-bearing capacity, keep adding weight until it fails. When testing longevity, run duty cycles until it breaks down. If you only "test to pass" your specifications, you don't really know how far away you are from a bad design. This is why toxicology tests sometimes involve feeding massive amounts of a new drug to animals. They have to find LD50—the amount that kills 50 percent of the animals. For a product with low toxicity, that number may literally be the physical limit of the animal's digestive system. A new drug needs a lot of margin between the amount needed to treat the target condition and the amount that will produce intolerable side effects.

- **Test to find more than one solution** that meets the requirements, so that you have more flexibility. If you learn something later that indicates a problem with the solution that you chose, you won't be held back, because you'll have another option.

These principles may seem to contradict the idea that we want our models to be fast and cheap. But think of it in reverse: if your models are fast and cheap, it won't cost as much to run through ten options or ten points in a range. It's not likely that you will able to build ten product variants. But you can have your 3D printer make ten different variants of a component design to help you understand the trade-offs for a design element. You can change the key values in your simulation and run it again. With today's tools, your major investment is in developing the first model. Once you have it, you might as well make the most of it to build more knowledge and make a better decision.

That knowledge is even more powerful when you use simple tools to make the knowledge easy to communicate and leverage: trade-off and limit curves.

Trade-Off and Limit Curves for Extensible Knowledge

Trade-off and limit curves are X-Y charts that visualize the knowledge you create when you test a range of solutions or test to failure. They show the limits of your design as it is currently conceived: The load-bearing arm can range between 6.12 meters and 7.29 meters long without adding reinforcement at the connection to the base. If it's too short, the payload hits the base. If it's too long, the arm is too heavy and breaks off under load.

The graph shows the upper and lower boundaries for this key dimension of the design, highlighting the safe region in between.

These are areas of product design that benefit from trade-off and limit curves:

- **Trade-offs within product platform designs that will be leveraged into multiple products or multiple customizations.** In this case, you know in advance that your product will be extended. If you are developing a Minimum Viable Product (MVP), you know that the product will need to be improved. When you understand the limits of your platform design, you know where it can be modified most easily and improved most readily.

- **Areas of the product where there is high risk of failure, high impact of failure or an untested idea, even if it's perceived to have low risk.** When you understand the trade-offs, you have room to maneuver. If the unexpected happens, you won't have to do as much work to find a different solution.

- **Areas of the product where there are core trade-offs to explore:** Strength vs. weight, volume vs. noise, concentration vs. performance and cost vs. anything. In these cases, just a little more work up front can help you find the optimal point of the trade-off curve for your specific design. Then if the parameters change—for your product or a future product—you've already done the work to know where to find the new optimum.

This is the way the Wright Brothers designed their first airplane so that they could fly it safely the first time. I'm no aerospace engineer, but I can read these curves. It's one way to capture the knowledge you have created so that you can share it with others.

Sharing the Knowledge You've Built

Most of the knowledge generated by a traditional product development team gets stuck in the developers' heads. They use it to make decisions, but they don't share it. The traditional Product Development Process (PDP) does not encourage them to share it. The traditional PDP includes only the deliverables needed for downstream partners to make, sell and support the product. When someone disagrees with a decision and wants to revisit it, it's hard to push back. When something doesn't work as expected, it's hard to figure out why. When the next product development program starts, the team has only its own experience to draw from.

With the Rapid Learning Cycles framework, a team does not have time to argue about things it has already learned. Instead, it documents its knowledge in real time, as it creates the knowledge, so that it's available to the rest of the team and to other teams working on similar problems. The Knowledge Gap and Key Decision Reports are designed to minimize the time required to capture your team's knowledge and decisions. The formats vary a lot, but they all have these elements in common:

- **One page to summarize the Knowledge Gap or Key Decision, the method used to close it, the results and the recommendation.** All of the important information needs to be visible at one time without flipping a page or changing slides. Limiting the report to one page forces the author to focus on the most important information.

- **Limited backup.** Raw data tables and analysis worksheets can be attached to the report with hyperlinks, in case anyone needs the detail. Single-slide reports can have a few slides with more details. If you don't give teams a firm limit for the number of slides, these reports degenerate into standard slide sets with fragmented knowledge. I coach my teams to allow no more than two slides in addition to the report.

Knowledge Gap Results	PROGRAM NAME
Owner:	Knowledge Gap Number
Learning Cycle:	• Font size at least 12 pt
	• No more than two additional slides

| The Question to Answer | What We Have Learned |

| The Purpose (link back to the Knowledge Gap's Key Decision) | |

| What We Have Done | Recommendations and Next Steps |

Figure 1.4: The Knowledge Gap Report

- **Quick to find and quick to read.** The team library is organized to make the reports easy to find. The format makes them easy to read. No one likes wading through a fifty-page report to find the single number that matters to them.

- **Captures the history in the same file.** If a Knowledge Gap or Key Decision gets discussed in more than one event, the document just gets copied into the same file (a new slide, tab or page) with the most recent one on top. A new team member can understand the history by reading the reports in sequence.

- **Uses graphics, charts and data tables with ease, and controls where they appear on the page.** Visual models cut down on the need for words and give more depth to the knowledge being shared. I like to use presentation software to make these reports, even if they are designed to be printed instead of projected. The author can finely control graphics placement and easily integrate

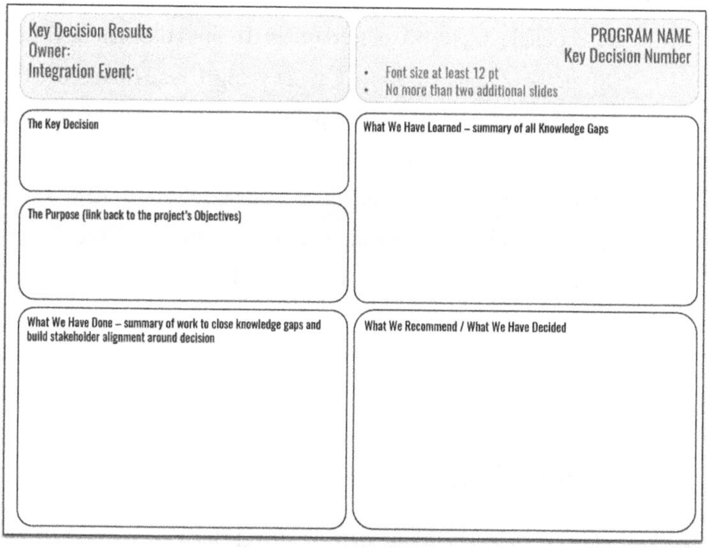

Key Decision Results Owner: Integration Event:	PROGRAM NAME Key Decision Number • Font size at least 12 pt • No more than two additional slides
The Key Decision	**What We Have Learned – summary of all Knowledge Gaps**
The Purpose (link back to the project's Objectives)	
What We Have Done – summary of work to close knowledge gaps and build stakeholder alignment around decision	**What We Recommend / What We Have Decided**

Figure 1.5: The Key Decision Report

tables and charts. Word processors make that too difficult, and spreadsheets make everything too gridlike.

It does take some practice to write a good report. Here are a few things to coach your team to do to make the learning curve shorter:

- **Present conclusions and recommendations, not data and analysis.** The person responsible for closing the Knowledge Gap should close the Knowledge Gap. This means doing more than just running the model and collecting the data. The person should feel and be empowered to draw conclusions. He or she is the one in the best position to do that. This should also be the person making the presentation—not the person's manager.

- **Use visual models instead of text and numbers wherever possible.** Present all data in graphical from. Mock-up drawings, photos and even video can all be embedded into the report if they help the audience understand the conclusions and recommendations.

- **Present quickly and leave most of the time for discussion.** Most people can read a lot faster than the presenter can talk. Take advantage of that by stating, "I'm not going to read this report, but here is the one thing I want to point out for you." They'll read the rest while you're talking.

It's wonderful to be able to stand up in front of your team, with a concise report and solid recommendations, to declare that you've closed a Knowledge Gap. But what do you do with all the Knowledge Gaps that you are not able to close?

What to Do with Unclosed Knowledge Gaps

By the end of the Kickoff Event, you will already have encountered some Knowledge Gaps that won't be closed. They have too little impact, or other Knowledge Gaps are much more important. So what do you do with these unclosed Knowledge Gaps? You don't throw them away, erase them or forget about them.

You continue to track them in your Knowledge Gaps backlog until the related Key Decisions have been made. Maybe a window of opportunity will open up to close them. You may find that your work to close another Knowledge Gap develops some information that makes them irrelevant.

When the Last Responsible Moment passes to make the related Key Decision, the team will have to make that decision with the Knowledge Gap still open. They will need to use their experience to make a judgement call based on their best assumptions.

Any unclosed Knowledge Gaps become risks. The program is at risk because those assumptions may be wrong, and if so, the product will suffer the consequences. In fact, the risk may be so grave that the team makes the Key Decision provisionally so that the product can continue moving toward launch while the team continues its work to close the Knowledge

Gaps. That way, it will know earlier if it has made a wrong turn, and can limit the damage.

Some unclosed Knowledge Gaps are important enough to justify the pursuit of multiple alternatives at once. This may seem like an expensive, unworkable strategy for a team that needs to conserve cash. But there are times when a little bit of convergence goes a long way.

CHAPTER ELEVEN

Convergent Decision Making

The previous chapter described how to close Knowledge Gaps using Design–Experiment–Capture, and that is all you need for 80 percent of them.

However, some Key Decisions are so critical to the success of the program that they are worth more investment to ensure that the decision does not have to be revisited later. These Key Decisions often relate to the customer, business and technical aspects of the Core Hypothesis:

- **Customer:** How will the customer use our product? What will be the user experience? Which specific customer persona will we design for first?
- **Business:** How will customers find the product? How much will they pay for it? How will they pay for it?
- **Technical:** What are the core components of the architecture? Who are the key suppliers and partners we need? What are we doing to differentiate ourselves from similar products?

These strategic decisions set the direction for the overall program, and so our temptation is to make them early and hope for the best. In the Rapid Learning Cycles framework, however, we pull learning earlier and push decisions later. For extremely important decisions like these, we take this to extremes. We maximize learning early and delay decisions as late as possible by pursuing multiple alternatives at once. This may sound expensive and difficult, but the benefits far outweigh the costs, and a few simple rules keep the complexity from getting out of hand.

What makes a decision ripe for convergence? When there are a number of competing alternatives, there is not enough good information to make a decision about the best one, and the consequences of a wrong decision are severe.

What Is Convergence?

Convergence is a method for making a complex decision by investigating multiple alternatives and narrowing down to the final solution in a series of steps. First, you establish a set to explore. Then you define a series of tests to probe the set for weaknesses. Each test will eliminate some options until you have found your final solution.

Convergence arose from Allen Ward's theoretical work to prove a method he called Set-Based Concurrent Engineering (SBCE). Ward demonstrated mathematically that a team is more likely to find a solution to an engineering challenge before it runs out of time if it pursues multiple alternatives at once (set-based). He envisioned that teams would use this process across multiple subsystems on overlapping problems to help them identify design conflicts earlier (concurrent engineering).

Ward's approach to SBCE is complex and difficult to implement in a team of any size. But I have experienced a lot of success with Convergence, which is a simplified version of SBCE. Convergence strips SBCE down to focus on one decision. That eliminates the need for a lot of the coordination work that makes SBCE unwieldy.

We converge on a decision in a series of stages. In the early stages, we evaluate large sets of alternatives using simple filters. As the set narrows, the tests become more complex until we arrive at the final solution.

Through convergence, we build our knowledge about the alternatives as we zoom in on the options that will work.

The stages have a simple structure: design the test, run the test, eliminate the weak. The process of running the test requires the team to refine the ideas, turning sketches into drawings and then simulations and prototypes. By sequencing these steps to accelerate the cheap and fast while delaying the expensive ones, we can avoid investing heavily in ideas that don't work.

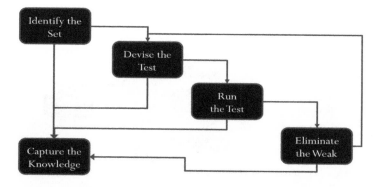

Figure 11.1: The Convergence Process

We Invest Only in Ideas That Work

With the teams I've coached, I've seen this scenario over and over again: the option that a team would have chosen at the beginning gets eliminated when a weakness is exposed. Another option emerges as the one that delivers the best performance with the fewest risks. Sometimes the results are even more surprising: an existing solution just needs some adjustment to outperform every new idea, or a far-out alternative with huge upside proves to be much more realistic than it appeared in the first round.

On the surface, Convergence seems to require a lot of additional time and resources. If you think of it as parallel path development, you would be right. But that's not what convergence is. The set of alternatives grows smaller until the Last Responsible Moment to make the final decision. Only the final concepts get full development.

Managers often balk at Convergence because they see only the work that goes into the alternatives that do not get selected. It seems wasteful to them to do anything that doesn't end up in the final product. However, they don't see all the effort that teams have to spend fixing things when the first choice does not work and they have no alternative.

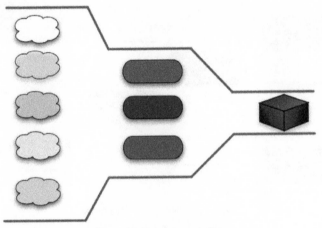

Figure 1.6: Convergence in Time

You may not believe this yourself. You can use the Rapid Learning Cycles framework without Convergence. But I challenge you to choose a difficult, recurring problem and apply some Convergence to it. If the problem is bad enough, it's easy to justify the resources to solve it permanently. When Convergence leads to a better solution in less time, and the knowledge gained keeps the team from having to solve the problem again in the next version of the product, Convergence will prove itself to you.

Prerequisites for Convergence

Convergence is a powerful tool, but it can easily go wrong if the team's not prepared for it. Convergence is demanding for the developers, difficult to manage for the Program Leader and stretches the limits of your organizational systems. So why bother with it at all? Because for some problems, there is no better way to make sure that the final solution is the one that will fully realize your vision for the product.

In order to succeed with Convergence, teams need to be able to do some things that completely break the rules of traditional product development:

- **Define good sets across functional boundaries.** A Convergence process is only as good as the set that converges. The team will need to learn how to work together to build sets that have safe options and wild card options, and sets that allow the team to understand the full design space.

- **Work in a coordinated fashion across subsystems to reduce the sets in a series of stages that do converge.** Convergence cannot happen in silos. Since we use Convergence only on major decisions, we almost always need a broad cross section of people to participate fully in the process, from designing the steps to designing the test to making narrowing decisions.

- **Recognize and surface conflicts as early as possible, which means paying more attention to other subteams.** Convergence surfaces conflicts. Teams that are not in alignment will have difficulty with every piece of the process. Sometimes you will need to work with subteams to get them aligned with one another before Convergence can start.

- **Delay decisions until the Last Responsible Moment—and push the Last Responsible Moment even later.** Convergence takes time, but it should not take an unbounded amount of time—a deadline for the Last Responsible Moment helps greatly. That deadline needs to be as late as possible, however. Your downstream partners can help with this by agreeing to work with partial information, work with a set of final candidates instead of a final answer and reduce their own lead times.

- **Eliminate the weak options to avoid reducing the set too soon.** We don't pick the strongest options to move forward—we remove the weakest options from the set of alternatives.

If this is your first attempt to use the Rapid Learning Cycles framework, you may be better off taking another look at this concept after you've had some experience closing Knowledge Gaps. You can also choose the single area of the product that keeps you up at night most often for your program, and run Convergence in that area.

Even after you have mastered Convergence, it is not something to attempt to do on the entire product program. It's only for the most risky areas, with the lowest visibility into the solution space. In those areas, the five Laws of Convergence will work to keep the uncertainty from overwhelming the team.

The Five Laws of Convergence

SBCE is a sophisticated way to solve complex challenges. The five Laws of Convergence make the complexity manageable so that the process moves steadily toward successful convergence while building the organization's knowledge for future decisions. These laws ensure that the method leads to a good result the first time:

- The First Law: Choose a good first set.
- The Second Law: Eliminate the weak.
- The Third Law: Take one more step.
- The Fourth Law: Stay within the set.
- The Fifth Law: Share the knowledge.

These laws work together to help the team manage the convergence process with a minimum of confusion and miscommunication.

First Law of Convergence: Choose a Good First Set

There are a number of ways to establish the first set of alternatives. You can brainstorm a list and then choose the ten that look the best. You can use decision tables to narrow your list down to the best candidates. Or you can set out from the beginning to build extensible knowledge: what is the best set to represent the potential solution space as we understand it? You may add some unlikely solutions to find the limits of the system, or you may consciously choose options that represent the range of alternatives that you have.

Here are different ways to define your set:

- **Set of discrete alternatives.** A number of options that are unrelated except that they are all possible solutions. Example: Ten different carbon fiber vendors.

- **Points within a range.** A number of options that represent different values within a continuous range. Example: Ten different concentrations of hydrochloric acid between 2 percent and 6 percent to find the optimal concentration to maximize performance.

- **Design variants.** A number of design options that differ from one another in a specific way to explore the design space. Example: Ten different cups with the same design but made from different paper, to minimize heat transfer and cost while maximizing compostability.

- **Nominal values with variation.** When making physical prototypes, you can take advantage of normal manufacturing variation to generate sets of alternatives. Ask your prototype component provider to produce a part based on nominal values for key dimensions without tolerances. The normal variation inherent in their manufacturing process will lead to parts with different combinations of key dimensions that you can test. Finalize the design based on the parts that work.

Any of these approaches will give you a number of alternatives to take through the process. Along the way, you may merge some of them together to get an even better alternative as you probe the set for weaknesses.

Feel free to include one or two wild card options that seem a little crazy. If they don't work, you'll quickly find out. But if they do work, you will be able to incorporate them into your product design with confidence that you could not have obtained without this process.

It's also helpful to include at least one safe option in your set. This is an option that works but perhaps not as well as you would like. It's like wearing khaki pants and a solid blue dress shirt to a casual workplace: it's acceptable but not exciting.

Your safe option could be the solution that was used on last year's product. It could be a low-performance solution that has a lot of margin for error. Given a choice, you would rather do something that pushes the envelope, but this option would do.

You can eliminate this option as soon as you have the same degree of confidence in another option that you like better. Even then, if something goes wrong, the safe option is there for you.

Second Law of Convergence: Eliminate the Weak

This is the most difficult law for people to get. Our default behavior, especially if we have an innovator mindset, is to choose the winners. We like working with the ideas that seem to have the most promise. We like making decisions and locking down options. It feels like progress.

When we choose the strongest options to go forward, we focus on the strengths that we see to find the ideas that perform the best. We forget that good performance on one test does not guarantee that the option will perform well on every test. It's easy to overlook weaknesses because we are not looking for them. If we are looking for winners, that's what we find.

However, when we are converging down to a solution from a set of alternatives, we get better results if we eliminate the weak and carry forward every alternative that passes our tests. We preserve maximum flexibility to find the best solution. Alternatives that barely passed early tests may be the strongest at the end, while the others may have fallen away.

We learn a lot more about the alternatives in our set when we focus on finding weaknesses. When we probe our ideas with a skeptical eye, we are much more likely to uncover hidden problems. When we establish tests that help us find weaknesses, we learn more about the entire set.

For example, I learn a lot more from a customer if I ask her to tell me what she doesn't like about the five alternatives I've put in front of her. That's especially true if I am presenting something that she's never seen before. The kinds of people who are willing to help with customer testing are people who generally like seeing new things. They may love everything we put in front of them, because it's new and we've tried to make it look nice for them. Some people are inclined to be polite and say only positive things unless we ask them for critical feedback. When we ask them what they don't like, we give them permission to give us their true opinions.

From a technical perspective, we learn so much more from failures than we do from successes. We learn the most from the failures we didn't expect: the option that has looked the greatest for weeks is the one with the lowest score. Our natural inclination is to ask ourselves why. The answers to that question make it possible for us to merge the best aspects of the solution that failed into a solution that passed, to get a stronger third alternative.

Convergence works best when each step is a hurdle that alternatives must pass.

Third Law of Convergence: Take One More Step

Each step in Convergence raises the bar that the alternatives must pass over, and develops them at the same time. At each step, we make an incremental investment to develop the ideas and then apply a new filter. We move from steps that require small investments to ones that require large investments. I like to map out the sequence that the team will follow to converge on a solution but retain the freedom to adjust it later. A good sequence has these characteristics:

- Fast tests go before slow tests.
- Cheap tests go before expensive tests.
- Each test requires the characterization of the item in the set to mature a bit. For example, you may move from sketches to drawings to 3D to prototypes.
- Each test is likely to fail at least 20 percent of the options.
- The tests generate extensible knowledge—not just pass/fail data.

For a Key Decision that involves the customer experience, we might follow a sequence like this:

- Observe customers as they go about their day, in the environment where they expect to use the product. Use this research to develop some alternatives.
- Make simple whiteboard sketches to illustrate the customer experience for the alternatives, then test the results by interviewing a handful of customers. Eliminate the ones that are hard to explain to the customers.
- Write user stories to flesh out the sketches, then test the results by acting out the user stories with your technical team. Eliminate the ones that are difficult to act out.
- Storyboard the user stories and show the storyboards to a new set of customers. Eliminate the ones that don't flow well.
- Prototype the user experience, using 3D printing to make models if necessary. Bring in a few more customers to have them test out

the user experience, and eliminate the ones that customers don't like.

- Build an MVP for a set of beta customers, and use split testing to get their reactions to the remaining alternatives. Eliminate the ones that cause users to make the most mistakes or generate the most frustration.

Here is a sequence for a Key Decision regarding a technical challenge:

- Brainstorm possible solutions, and use a decision table to get down to five candidates.
- Make simple study drawings, either by hand or in a drawing tool, then discuss to find the weakest alternative. Eliminate it.
- Cut some models out of cardboard and put them together to see if they are interacting in the way you expect. Eliminate any options that don't work.
- Draw up the parts and send them to a 3D printer. Put them together and then review them with a manufacturing engineer to get some preliminary cost estimates. Eliminate the options that exceed your cost budget for the parts.
- Send the final two candidates to your manufacturing group for a test run. Assuming that they both could pass validation testing, choose the one with the better cost structure. But keep the other one in your back pocket just in case.

At every step, the ideas become more and more concrete and integrated into the overall design.

Fourth Law of Convergence: Stay Within the Set

The process is complex enough without adding new ideas to the set. Yet this is another big temptation for innovators that we have to resist. Once the process of Convergence has begun, we do not add new alternatives to the set unless it becomes absolutely necessary—if we have a test that none of our alternatives can pass. Even then, we must subject new alternatives to the same convergence path that the other alternatives have already traveled.

This is how we keep ourselves and our partners from going crazy with this process. If you are constantly moving alternatives in and out of the set, others around you cannot depend upon your decisions. Your own team members lose track of what's in and what's out. It's difficult to converge when the set continues to diverge.

If you have a great idea and the testing has already begun, your product is almost always better off if you put the idea into a "parking lot" for the next version of the product, as long as you have a set with at least one viable alternative. It's not worth the disruption to add it. Worse, if you get into the habit of adding options in the middle of the process, people will not trust the process and it will break down.

We can merge two alternatives into one, and we can take something that works well in one alternative and apply it to all the others to see if it enhances them. If the idea exists in the current set and has made it all the way through testing, it's probably OK.

Fifth Law of Convergence: Share the Knowledge

Running a Convergence process involves some extra overhead. We recoup it through our ability to find a better solution, and by preserving flexibility to allow ourselves to make better decisions. You can test this by identifying the top option in the set at the beginning—the one you would pick if you were forced to make a choice. Then monitor what happens to it throughout the process. I have yet to see one that did not get either eliminated along the way, or substantially strengthened by incorporating elements of the other alternatives. But this is only the beginning of the value that a well-designed Convergence process can generate.

When we choose sets to help us fully understand the ranges of alternative solutions to a problem, we develop extensible knowledge. We may develop a solution that applies to other products. We may use the knowledge we gained to evolve the product in a future version. We may develop trade-off and limit curves that help us share this knowledge with other teams. We may have developed new models that can shorten decision-making time for future programs.

The Convergence process is not complete until this knowledge has been shared. In the Rapid Learning Cycles framework, this sharing happens naturally through the Knowledge Gap and Key Decision reports. New models may be incorporated into templates that others can use. New test methods can be shared among teams.

Mistakes People Make with Convergence

Because Convergence is so counterintuitive, it has some known failure points where our normal behavior gets in the way of a good result. Here are the five major reasons why a Convergence process fails to deliver a better solution:

- **The initial set was too broad.** If your set is too big, even the early, fast, cheap tests will take a long time to run. Scale the size of your sets to the amount that you can do within a single learning cycle. Some types of simulations are easy to run for a lot of alternatives, but you may need to restrict the set size for the physical tests that you will need later. It's hard to juggle too many alternatives mentally when the team is discussing them and trying to narrow them. I know of few situations that require more than ten options in the initial set. Five is more typical, and three is probably too few to get good Convergence.

- **The team did more work than necessary to eliminate the options.** Once you know that an option is not a good fit, the team's time is better spent working on something else. You want to do the minimum amount of work necessary to differentiate among the alternatives in the set. Otherwise, the Convergence process will be too expensive for the value it creates. Sometimes this issue leads people to view Convergence as a method that costs too much, and so they fail to use it on the Knowledge Gaps that need it the most.

- **The team chose the strongest option.** I described why it was important to eliminate the weak options. When a team chooses the strong options instead, it misses signs that its preferred alternatives are weaker than they seem. That can lead the team to select a final option that has some significant deficits that the team doesn't see until it's too late.

- **The team reopened the set to new options.** If you continuously open up your set to new options, you don't have a convergence funnel—you have a blob that your team can't get its arms around. The option set keeps changing shape. The team and downstream partners can't keep up, and the chances of getting a good solution go down dramatically. Since the process isn't working as it was designed, the team abandons it midway through and just picks something to stop the chaos from getting worse.

- **The team converged too quickly, before the decision needed to be made.** This reduces flexibility in an area of the product where you need it the most. It's better to time the narrowing steps so that the final decision happens at the Last Responsible Moment, so that the team can take advantage of all the knowledge built around the decision.

When you have run a single Convergence process without running into these problems, you are ready to try it across multiple subteams.

Convergence Across Multiple Subteams

In the beginning of this chapter, I said that it was difficult to run Convergence on overlapping problems. I certainly don't recommend that you start out that way. But once you've gained some experience with Convergence and start to see the benefits, more and more opportunities will arise to apply it. Eventually, some of these will overlap.

This overlapping process requires strict adherence to the five Laws of Convergence, and good communication between the teams. Their convergence sequences need to be coordinated, so that they make their narrowing decisions in step with each other. Normally, these narrowing steps take place during a Learning Cycle or Integration Event, with all of the affected team members in the room. Their task is to be sure that none of the remaining options conflict with the options in other sets. Otherwise, it is too easy for one team to eliminate the only options that work for another team.

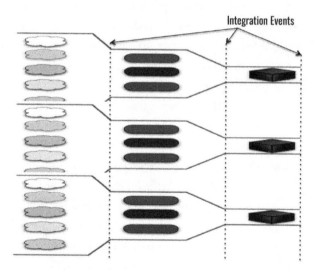

Figure 1.7: Convergence Across Subsystems

When your teams reach this level of maturity, your job is to coordinate the convergence across multiple teams. You will need to help each team design its sequence, and then integrate all of the sequences into a Master Convergence Plan. You will need to make sure that the other work to close Knowledge Gaps and make Key Decisions is timed to fit into the Master Convergence Plan. You will also need to make sure that Convergence is reserved for the Knowledge Gaps and Key Decisions that are critical to the success of the project—the ones for which this is the best chance to find a good solution.

What If There Is No Solution?

Sometimes a narrowing decision results in an empty set: none of the options passed the test. The temptation is to say that the process failed and start over, this time choosing the option the team likes the best but hasn't validated. They need your help to avoid that temptation. Instead, they need to use the knowledge they have just built to figure out what needs to change so that they can find a solution.

Here are three alternatives that the team can pursue instead:

- **Step backward in the Convergence process to find the next best solution, and strengthen it until it passes all the tests.** Often the final tests are the ones that everything fails. They are the most demanding tests that best reflect real-world performance. To move forward, the team can walk backward in the Convergence process to find the next best alternative and figure out what it needs to do to strengthen the option. It may need to walk back to the place where the safe option was eliminated because the team believed another option was just as safe. It can think about how to strengthen the safe option so that it is a little more appealing.

- **Look for constraints that can be relaxed.** If none of the options can be strengthened so that it passes the tests, you need to look at the tests themselves. The team established the set, the tests and the narrowing decision criteria. Is it possible that those criteria can be opened up a bit, so that some of the rejected options stay in the set? This requires the team to think deeply about the reasons why it established the decision criteria that it did. What evidence does it have to support the need for the criteria that it established? Sometimes the team will find that if it relaxes a criterion just a little, a viable alternative pops back into the set.

- **Add to the set, but only as a last resort.** New alternatives are even more risky at this point. The team put a lot of its best thinking into the initial set, and ended up with nothing. It's possible that it learned something along the way that helped it find some new alternatives. But the team knows almost nothing about those alternatives. Those alternatives need to go through the same tests as the set that is now empty.

  That's why this is the most time-consuming and risky option, even though it may seem that this choice just requires some extra brainstorming. Given that you've already had one set of alternatives fail completely, it's likely that the second set will also end up empty unless you change something about the tests. But if you do change the tests, it's better to reevaluate the options that you already know very well, so that you don't need to disrupt the entire Learning Cycles Plan.

Convergence in the Learning Cycles Plan

We represent the Convergence process in the Learning Cycles Plan with a series of Knowledge Gaps that lead to a Key Decision. Each Knowledge

Gap represents a narrowing step. The Key Decision is the final narrowing step to get to one answer.

The narrowing steps take place either in or alongside the Learning Cycle Events. For simple Convergence on single decisions, it works better if the subteam makes the narrowing decision ahead of the Learning Cycle Event and then reports on it in the event. Usually these narrowing decisions are straightforward and don't require input from a lot of others. Even if you have multiple groups converging in parallel, only the people involved in the convergence need to participate in the decision. They are the ones closest to it because they are the ones responsible for the final Key Decision.

The rest of the team will see that the group starts with a full set of alternatives, and that each learning cycle whittles the set down until it reaches a final answer. You may need to help the team get comfortable working with partial information or more than one alternative until it reaches a final decision. The good news is that once these decisions get made, they stick. Since they are the most important decisions that you have to make for your product, Convergence can help ensure that the product you build is the one that you envisioned.

CHAPTER TWELVE

The Rapid Learning Cycles Program Leader

The Rapid Learning Cycles Program Leader is not a project manager. This is not a role for someone who is primarily interested in checklists, schedules and budgets.

You are the one responsible for the shortest distance between you and your new product. Whether you came up with the original idea or ran with an idea that was given to you, your mission is to turn that idea into reality.

Your product may slot well within your company's existing product lines, or you may be pursuing something disruptive. In addition to the product, you may need to build supply chains and distribution channels, partner relationships, new business models and perhaps even an entire company. It doesn't matter what it says on your business card. Your primary role is to be an entrepreneur—even if you work in a Fortune 500 company.

Program Leaders Drive the Vision

Program Leaders are the people responsible for developing product visions and then driving them out into the market. This role requires deep

Figure 12.1: The Rapid Learning Cycles Program Leader

customer, technical and business knowledge—or the willingness to get that knowledge. The Program Leaders are the ones responsible for putting the pieces together. They find the places where a new scientific discovery fulfills a customer's unmet need or a solution from one industry creates a market opportunity in another.

The person who founds a startup naturally plays the role of a Rapid Learning Cycles Program Leader. There is no Marketing team to define the customer, no Human Factors group to study user behavior, no financial analysts to build cost worksheets. The entrepreneur may eventually build a team that includes these people. But in the early days, during the drive to get funding and release the first product, a lot of this falls on the founder's shoulders.

Later, founders will need to turn this role over to other people, if they want to grow into executives capable of leading the whole company—or they may sell the company and repeat the process with something new. The Steve Jobses of the world find ways to never give up this role.

Program Leaders in Corporate R&D

Corporate R&D departments tend to make life difficult for natural Program Leaders. Traditional product development asks the Program Leader to be a project manager, responsible for managing schedules, budgets and stakeholders. In some organizations, project leaders may have no technical or marketing background at all. Instead, they are professional project managers with expert knowledge of sophisticated tools for managing large projects. The technical leadership comes from experienced engineers, while Marketing contributes customer knowledge. In some organizations, the Marketing department writes up the requirements for the engineers to execute and the project becomes a tug-of-war between what Marketing wants and what Engineering can deliver.

The Program Leader wants to spend as little time as possible on the formalities of project management. Instead, he or she wants to collaborate with technical, design, marketing and operations experts to produce the best possible product—the one that most closely realizes the Program Leader's vision for the product. In a traditional organization, a marketing- or design-centered program manager lacks credibility with the engineers—and the engineering-centered program manager tends to discount the potential contribution from marketing or design partners. Any of them will have trouble when it's time to talk to Operations. Meanwhile, the heavyweight PDP drags everybody down.

This has led to a lot of misguided advice over the years on how to support innovation in a corporate setting: by establishing skunkworks teams or separating business development activities from the rest of the organization. It's true that these so-called "intrapreneurs" need organizational support and a protected budget, and their very presence challenges the corporate power structure. But if you cut them out of the organization, you cut them off from the support services they need to bring the product all the way to market. Innovation should not be delegated, outsourced or cut off from the main flow of products. Instead, the organization should seek to grow the capacity to innovate across product development.

The Characteristics of a Program Leader

Program Leaders cultivate these attributes:

- **Systems perspective.** Program Leaders have the ability to see the entire product and its ecosystem, even when looking at only a small piece. They can make decisions that reflect their ultimate vision for the product even when the decisions themselves are small. They have the ability to communicate this understanding to others, so that most of the team's decisions are in alignment with the vision.

- **Customer empathy.** Program Leaders live and breathe customer value. It's easy to develop a product we want to buy ourselves. It's harder to develop a great product for someone who has an entirely different set of abilities, interests and needs. Program Leaders have the ability to build an understanding of the customer's perspective and see needs that the customers themselves cannot articulate. They seek to put themselves in the customer's environment.

- **Convergence mindset.** Program Leaders are comfortable with the uncertainty that is inherent in Convergence. They crave flexibility because it gives them more room to maneuver. They have the ability to delay decisions and to encourage others to delay them until the Last Responsible Moment. They will learn to recognize when it is time to converge so that the program stays on track.

- **Stakeholder awareness.** Program Leaders build strong relationships with the people who will be critical to the successful execution of the product vision. They understand that they have been given a great deal of responsibility and trust. Their team members' careers may rest in your hands. They take care to ensure that they have open lines of communication with partners, senior leaders and other key stakeholders so that the organization can stay aligned as the product vision evolves.

- **Courage and conviction.** Program Leaders develop bold product visions that push the organization's comfort zones, and advocate successfully for ideas. Once they have the go-ahead to execute the vision, they take responsibility for steering the vision through the development process, making tough decisions to get the best balance of customer and business value.

This can be a daunting list, but this role is one that you can grow into. Fortunately, you have a team of people who can help you.

Expert Team Coach

After driving the product vision, your next major role is to be your team's coach. Although you hold the product vision, you are probably not the expert on every aspect of your product. For example, even if you are the inventor and know the technology inside and out, you are probably not an expert on the customer segments to target and the best ways to reach them, or the legal strategies you need to protect your intellectual property. Even a solo entrepreneur needs some expert help.

Experts thrive when they are empowered to make and act on their own decisions and make their own plans. The Rapid Learning Cycles framework takes advantage of this to keep the team focused on learning vs. doing. The responsibility for defining activities is given to the person who is responsible for closing a Knowledge Gap. With an experienced team, you may need to spend very little time reviewing the details of their daily work.

At the same time, you are the one reading this book. You are the one who has decided that you will run this program within the Rapid Learning Cycles framework. You can give copies of this book to your entire team to read (I encourage that!). At the end of the day, however, someone will need to take responsibility for ensuring that the team lives into the framework. Someone has to schedule the Kickoff Event, Learning Cycle Events and Integration Events. Someone has to publish templates for Knowledge Gap and Key Decision Reports. Someone has to keep the Status Events on track. That someone is probably you.

I know you're not an expert on all of this just yet. You and your team will be learning together how to scope out your Key Decisions, Knowledge Gaps and activities. It will take some iterations to find the way to run events that works best within your company culture. Your team will probably need to experiment with different ways to close Knowledge Gaps and run Convergence processes.

You help them in five ways:

- **Learn yourself.** Admit to everyone that you want to try this out, but that you've never done it before. The ride will be a little bumpy at first while everyone learns together. Be the first person to recognize that an idea of yours didn't work out as expected. Show that you are open and willing to accept feedback, but not willing to go back to traditional product development.

- **Challenge the team.** Good coaches listen and ask questions. You don't need to be that far ahead of your team on the learning curve in order to ask questions like, "What do we already know about this?" "What evidence do you have of that?" "Who has overcome this challenge before?" or "What can we do to push this decision back another two weeks without disrupting the rest of the schedule?" When someone violates the team agreements about how Knowledge Gap reports will be prepared or what to say at a Status Event, don't let it slide. When you call them on it with respect, the entire team learns.

- **Continuously scan the landscape for the shortest path.** Remember that the shortest path consists of Key Decisions that you are able to make with the best available information, so that they don't create loopbacks later. As the person with the clearest big-picture view, you are the one in the best position to see if the team is working on the right Key Decisions and Knowledge Gaps. You don't want to jerk the team around by changing their focus every day. Before every Learning Cycle Event, it's helpful for you to spend some private time reflecting on the team's progress and where it needs to go next. The Learning Cycle Event is the place to steer the team to that shortest path.

- **Never stop talking about the vision.** You'll start talking about the vision before the Kickoff Event, when you are working with your organization to put together the right team. You'll use it to define the Core Hypothesis that you will present to the team at the Kickoff Event. You'll talk about it at every event. You'll use it as the touchstone to help you recognize when a Knowledge Gap has been closed and a Key Decision has been made so that it will stick. When you coach people, continue to bring them back to the vision. Your team members should be able to recite it in their sleep before the end.

- **Keep others out of the way.** If this is the first time your organization has run a program with Rapid Learning Cycles, a lot of people may try to interfere. The owners of the standard PDP, Operational Excellence black belts, Lean Office facilitators, senior leaders and middle managers will look at your program through the lenses of traditional product development, lean tools, project management "best practices" and operational excellence expectations. You are going in a different direction entirely. You help your team the most by insulating them from people who mean well but don't understand the framework and won't believe that it works until you show that it delivers results.

This brings us to the third most important role you play.

Stakeholder Liaison

Development programs have a lot of stakeholders. The PDP eventually touches nearly the entire organization in some way. It's clear that R&D and Marketing have a strong, if sometimes difficult, partnership. Operations groups will ultimately be responsible for getting products to customers. The Finance group provides expertise to model costs and program profitability, while the IT and HR groups provide critical support functions such as bringing new team members on board as quickly as possible.

If you work in a large, structured R&D organization, you'll need to run some interference for your team. Functional partners outside the team will be expecting your team to run like every other team: late, slow and unpredictable at the end. You'll need to stay on top of them to ensure that they are ready when your team needs them. You will need their help to delay decisions and eliminate checklist items that the Rapid Learning Cycles framework addresses in a different way. Until they see it, they won't believe that your program will be different, and so you need to make an extra effort to communicate your team's progress and ask for help in removing barriers.

If you are an entrepreneur building your own company, you don't get to skip this section. Your stakeholders include your investors, Board of Directors, employees, outside regulatory bodies and even your family.

Much of your success will be driven by your ability to pull what you need from these people to build a strong organization.

Stakeholders don't like to be unpleasantly surprised, and they like to be consulted on decisions that affect them. Stakeholders who are higher than you in the organizational hierarchy appreciate respect for their position in the company and the hard work that got them there. Stakeholders who are peers and subordinates appreciate respect for their expertise and experience. Even the newest of the new hires brings something to the table, or you would not have hired her.

To be a good stakeholder liaison, you need to spend time with your stakeholders and reach out to them before you need them. They need to trust you, and they need to know exactly what you need from them, even if they are not trustworthy and are opaque about what they need from you. This is especially important in the Rapid Learning Cycles framework because you and your team do not have slack time for dealing with miscommunications, mismatched expectations and unreasonable stakeholder demands. You will be asking them to participate in making Key Decisions at the Last Responsible Moment and then sticking with those decisions, even if that is not the way programs typically go inside your organization.

If the role of stakeholder liaison is not comfortable to you, consider finding a coach or a mentor who can help you with it. Many engineers and scientists find that this aspect of program leadership is not natural. But it is a learnable skill, and if you care enough about your program's success, you will stretch yourself to master it. A good job here reduces many of the risks that demand your response.

Risk Responder

In Part Two, I described the importance of risk management, especially risks that arise when the team can't close Knowledge Gaps in time. No matter how you keep track of your risks, it is your responsibility to take care of them.

As the Program Leader, you are the one with the best grasp of the system-level product. This means that you are also in the best position to identify and respond to the most important risks that your program faces. Risk responder is not a natural role for most innovators, who want to think only about the work that remains to realize the product vision. We're naturally focused on the product's upside, and the closer the product gets to launch, the more excited we are about the possibilities for the product.

Chances are, there are people on your team who are good risk identifiers. They look at the product and see all the things that could go wrong. It's easy to dismiss them, but it's better to use them as your allies to help you stay on top of the biggest risks. They can help you prioritize the risks and allocate the resources you have to close Knowledge Gaps that mitigate and eliminate risk. They can remind you that adding a new feature just before a major validation test is probably not a good idea, even if it looks as though everything will be OK.

This role is difficult for me too. I always think everything will work out. My business partner is the one who scans the landscape for all the things we need to avoid. After I've run out of rationalizations to explain why his concerns are not valid, we work together to develop plans that are more robust. The plans account for the uncertainties that we face, no matter how thoroughly we have closed Knowledge Gaps and no matter how well-informed our Key Decisions may be.

Ultimately, risk response is in your court. You are the one who has the charge to get the product out. There is nothing more frustrating than being close to launch and then discovering something that sets you back weeks or months. Good risk response can't eliminate this scenario entirely, but it can make it much less likely. The risks will be much easier to manage if you have backup.

The Support You Need to Thrive

Your organization may not be fully prepared to support you in this creative, dynamic role. The Rapid Learning Cycles framework will help it support you by giving structure to your team's work in early development, and by making your progress toward a product a lot more visible.

If this is the first program to use Rapid Learning Cycles at your company or division, you need someone who can remove barriers and advocate for you. You will be able to work a lot more efficiently if you have an executive-level sponsor who understands and supports your intention to use the Rapid Learning Cycles framework.

This should be a person who sees the value of getting the company's best ideas to market faster and is willing to help you try out this framework. Ideally, the sponsor is able to perceive success even if everything does not go perfectly the first time, since there is a learning curve for you and the team.

Here are some specific requests you can make of your sponsor that will increase your effectiveness immediately:

- **Permission to push decisions later and pull learning earlier.** This framework may require you to make major adjustments to the PDP gate expectations. If you are pushing decisions later, you won't have final answers for some things when your PDP expects them. For example, specifications tend to float for several months after the normal deadline, and they won't be finalized all at once. Each spec will be defined when the team is at the Last Responsible Moment to define it. If your PDP expects approved specifications at the second gate, you should let your sponsor know that you won't have them yet.

- **A protected budget for the next phase of the program.** It's unreasonable and unnecessary to expect the entire development budget for the program to be protected at the beginning of the program. But the team needs stability until the end of the current phase of development, and some assurance that the next phase will be funded, too. Every program gets hurt by budget cuts that eliminate funds for experimentation, travel restrictions that prevent team members from meeting with partners, and resource reallocations that destabilize the team. The Rapid Learning Cycles framework exacerbates these harms, because the team depends upon resources being available to build the knowledge it needs to create. If a Knowledge Gap needs to be closed but the money's not there, the team is in a worse situation than if it had guessed, because it is being forced to guess without as much time available to recover if it guesses wrong.

- **Waivers for deliverables that don't make sense for the team.** If the team does a great job working with Operations partners to identify and close Knowledge Gaps, it may not need as many Design-for-Manufacturability reviews. It may not need to hold a specific event to get this feedback, because it has been getting the feedback all along. Some risk management deliverables won't make sense, and the program schedule will be run completely differently than it is in a traditional program.

- **Air cover to explore innovative approaches.** The more traditional your PDP has been, the more likely you are to bump up against functional partners who expect your team to work in the usual way. Quality, Regulatory and Legal departments and Procurement teams may balk the most about delaying decisions, working with partial information and omitting status reports and documentation. Your sponsor can help you identify and work through these objections early to find alternative methods of communication that work for both groups.

- **A dedicated team room.** If you have the space, it's helpful for the team to have a dedicated conference room or other space. This space is where the team can always see the Learning Cycles Plan, Knowledge Gap Reports and Key Decisions Reports. It's a place where they can keep prototypes out on the table, and system models on the walls. They will hold their Status and Learning Cycle Events in the room, and get together for impromptu discussions.

With these measures in place, you're set to begin driving the vision, as long as you are personally prepared to be the leader your team needs you to be.

Team Stabilizer

Finally, consider taking a look in the mirror. Are you the one who can't wait to get your hands on the next build, even if that's not the best way to close the most important Knowledge Gap? Do you feel uncomfortable leaving things open, and push for decisions to be locked down early?

Are you the one who encourages your team to add options to the set after it has converged? Are you the one who wants to revisit decisions after the Last Responsible Moment? Does your vision for the product change constantly, leaving your teammates breathless as they run to keep up with you?

The Rapid Learning Cycles framework can't help you if you perpetuate the problems of traditional product development. If you grew up in that environment, you have some behaviors to unlearn, so that new behaviors can replace them.

If you've never developed a product before, you need to remember that our instinctual approach to product development is also not the shortest path. Convergence, the Last Responsible Moment and learning before doing are all counterintuitive, especially when it's so easy to just write out some code or grab a part off a 3D printer.

If you're like most innovators I know, you'll do anything ethical to get your product to market, including developing yourself into the Program Leader that your team and your product need you to be.

PART FOUR

Rapid Learning Cycles
in the
Product Development Organization

CHAPTER THIRTEEN

The Lean Startup with Rapid Learning Cycles

I n Chapter Three, I outlined some assumptions for the generic program that used the Rapid Learning Cycles framework. I assumed that the program was at the beginning, and that you were the Program Leader. I assumed that you had a team, and that you had a preexisting PDP that you needed to fit into. I assumed that the product was new—that you had a Core Hypothesis that needed validation, a number of significant Key Decisions to make and Knowledge Gaps to close.

In the next two chapters, I'll describe how to use this framework if those assumptions are not true. I'll describe the types of products that are probably not good fits for this method—where the industry either has something that works just as well or where the adaptation required is just too big. Finally, I'll cover how to use this framework if you are not at the beginning of the program, but realize that you have some learning cycles that need to be done to prevent some major loopbacks.

The "How" to the Lean Startup's "What"

Eric Ries, the author of *The Lean Startup* is a startup veteran. He learned from his failures and successes that just a little process rigor goes a long way, when the team is small, time and money are in short supply and investors want to see results. His book defines some of the key things that an entrepreneur needs to do in order to validate her idea, according to measures that demonstrate real customer engagement, and he is not prescriptive about the process you need to get there.

The fact that most startups consist of small teams with rapid communication does not eliminate the need for clarity about the purpose of the work to be done and the challenges to be overcome, or the need for clear agreements about how the team will work together.

Ries provides the "what"—the Rapid Learning Cycles framework tells you "how" to implement his ideas. This book provides the operating system that entrepreneurs can use to structure their work without implementing a heavyweight, inflexible process. The methods are well-defined and scalable to quick investigations or complex development programs.

The Lean Startup for Tangible Products

This chapter focuses on the challenges that face a startup team that is established to commercialize a tangible invention—a product that exists in the physical realm vs. the virtual or services realm. This means that the team will need to design the product for manufacturability and reliability, build a supply chain and distribution network, develop a quality plan, achieve regulatory approvals and certifications and develop sales channels.

This is not the original challenge that Lean Startup was designed to solve. Lean Startup was developed in an environment where most startup companies build either software products (apps, software-as-a-service offerings) or services (Uber, Airbnb). These products repackage components of known IT infrastructures to deliver services in new ways.

I don't want to discount the challenges these companies face. But these products differ from tangible products in these five ways:

- They don't carry physical inventory, which means that they don't have to deal with design interactions with supply chains and distribution that have long lead times.

- They can change their product relatively easily by updating the underlying software on a central server. This gives them the ability to release multiple product variants and new releases easily, and existing customers can benefit from changes as well as new customers.

- Their early adopter customers are forgiving. While the product does have to work well enough to gain traction, it usually doesn't have to work perfectly to be acceptable.

- Regulatory controls are not burdensome. These products don't require interaction with regulatory bodies such as the EPA, FDA or USDA or their counterparts in the European Union.

- They don't need to work in the physical realm, where the principles of physics, biology and chemistry apply.

For these reasons, the Lean Startup method and the Agile Development practices that underlie it are necessary but not sufficient, and require adaptation.

Your first tangible product has to be much more developed than a software or service product to be produced in quantities that are large enough to serve as a valid test of your Core Hypothesis. Even if you intend to make your first products with 3D printers and then sell them at local fairs, you'll find that you have a minimum quantity that you need to make in order to turn a profit at a price that a customer would pay.

Rapid Learning Cycles Make the Lean Startup Model Work Better

Steve Blank formulated the elements of the Lean Startup model during his time teaching Entrepreneurship at Stanford. His student Eric Ries encapsulated his experiences with this model into *The Lean Startup*. This model emphasizes a strong product vision, good measures that help teams understand product performance, and fast cycles of learning. Blank encouraged teams to release their Minimum Viable Product (MVP)—the most basic product that will deliver some piece of the product vision that a customer will pay for—and then iterate on it based on real customer feedback.

In fact, Blank runs his Entrepreneurship classes using cadenced cycles of learning. Teams must talk with potential customers in between weekly classes and report on their experiences in class. This creates pull for the students to get the customer interviews done. They have a one-week learning cycle.

Even if you are working on a new type of web service, you will get more value out of your customer investigations if you know what Key Decisions you need to make and what Knowledge Gaps you need to close. The real difference is that a software or services startup can build a prototype and then quickly transform it into a product that can form the basis for experimentation with a growing customer base.

In the physical world, we run into the limitations of our physical models, distribution channels and support challenges before we get to a point where we can sell more than a handful. With these products, it's essential that we make good Key Decisions that stick because they are much less easy to undo later.

We can experiment with our customers, but we need to be more conscious about the ramifications for product safety, long-term support and maintenance for our first products, and relations with manufacturing and distribution partners.

Rapid Learning Cycles Channel the Entrepreneur's High Energy to Maximize Value

Entrepreneurs succeed because they have the energy to turn their great ideas into great products. The downsides are that entrepreneurs tend to run quickly in a lot of directions at once and the energy often comes from being in love with their ideas.

Rapid Learning Cycles help us channel our desire to jump into action into the research and experimentation that will help us learn faster.

- The framework emphasizes the need to validate the Core Hypothesis that underlies the product idea and the major decisions that drive the product's success or failure. This shakes out bad ideas and strengthens good ones.

- The framework structures the program with rapid experimentation to develop the knowledge your team needs to make major decisions and capture that knowledge so that new team members can come up to speed quickly on the product's history and current direction.

- The framework expands Build–Measure–Learn into a broader understanding of experimental design. Your team has alignment on the questions that each cycle is trying to answer, and then team members run only the appropriate tests to help them answer those questions as rapidly and cheaply as possible.

- The framework will help your team understand when to use models, when to build prototypes and when it's time to release the first MVP.

- The framework will help your team understand how to evolve the product from the MVP into a whole solution in a series of development cycles.

It helps to be in love with the idea that you're working long hours to bring to fruition, but entrepreneurs who don't temper that with real-world validation don't learn fast enough to deliver a great product before the time, money and goodwill runs out. Your investors, potential employees and partners, family members and customers want to see results to build their confidence in your ability to deliver.

Rapid Learning Cycles Build Confidence in the Startup Team

Even a startup team needs to build confidence. If you're in a startup, you don't have an established customer base to manage—but you do have to manage your investors' expectations as you secure funding and work toward delivering your first product. You need to be able to demonstrate that you're making progress. The faster you succeed at launching your product and the more successful that product is in the market, the more power you will have in your negotiations with those investors, and the more control you will retain over your vision for your product and your company.

The Rapid Learning Cycles framework gives you greater mastery over the challenges you need to overcome as you realize the vision for your new product. This mastery helps you project greater confidence and provide better information to potential investors. You'll have a deeper understanding of the strengths and weaknesses of your product idea, and therefore of what you will need to succeed with it.

This framework gives you just the right amount of structure to help you manage an environment of high uncertainty. It will help you prioritize your work so that you can conserve the money, time and goodwill that you depend upon until your first product proves itself. It will help you deliver that product faster and make your resources last longer to give you more running room so that you have more time to adapt as you learn.

The Rapid Learning Cycles Framework for Startups and Entrepreneurs

The concepts of Key Decisions and Knowledge Gaps help a startup team understand the dependencies between the different streams of experimentation that need to run simultaneously. The framework can help them understand which elements of the Core Hypothesis are the most risky, and which ones can be deferred until later.

We use Rapid Learning Cycles to structure the activities in the Lean Startup approach, with three major differences:

- **We resist the temptation to build things immediately.** Instead, we conduct small-scale experiments, such as customer interviews and observations, to help us learn about customer needs without investing in a product build. This is true even though things like iPad apps and online classes don't require months of work.

- **We use Design–Experiment–Capture instead of Build–Measure–Learn,** to make sure that we understand what we need to learn before we build anything, and so that we run all the cheap, easy experiments first before we invest in development work. Just a little bit of rigor to understand the question that needs answering, why it needs to be answered and how the experimental model will lead to an answer will help ensure that the team maximizes the value of the time and money it spends on experiments. In the Design step, the team may find that someone else already has an answer to the question.

- **We use Convergence to evaluate multiple alternatives for major Key Decisions.** Serial development takes too much time and money, and parallel path development is faster but too expensive. Decisions like channel strategies and distribution partners are a natural fit for convergence, because there are a lot of potential partners with different business models to evaluate.

Startup teams see strong benefit from a regular cadence. In the absence of a PDP with standard deliverables and expectations, the learning cycle cadence helps the team stay aligned and coordinated.

Learning cycles provide natural opportunities for the team to establish group norms around things like coding standards so that team members can cover for each other, test methods, infrastructure components like knowledge libraries and collaboration software.

In a startup environment, everyone is running as fast as they can. The Learning Cycle events provide space for the team to breathe, reflect and adjust before running off again.

Entrepreneurs Have Key Decisions and Knowledge Gaps on Every Aspect of the Business

We use Key Decisions and Knowledge Gaps to implement the major elements of the Lean Startup, to help us decide:

- What is the product's Core Hypothesis? (This is at the Strategy level in the Lean Startup framework.) How can we validate it?
- What does the MVP look like for the market we most want to reach?
- What does the roadmap look like to evolve the MVP until we have fully realized the product vision?
- What do we do ourselves, and what do we hire experts to do for us?
- What measures will help us assess the performance of the product?

Although this book has discussed Key Decisions and Knowledge Gaps from the perspective of the product, the framework can encompass much more than that. You can run learning cycles on the funding model, and on all the other aspects of establishing a business for the first time:

legal structures, hiring, team structures, office space, make vs buy decisions—anything where you have a major decision to make, and a lot of Knowledge Gaps to close.

If you're like most entrepreneurs, you want to spend as little time as possible on these things. Yet a poor decision can drain cash from your business and make it an unattractive place to work. Doing one or two learning cycles on all the administrative work can help you clear a lot of it out of the way so that you can focus on what you want to do the most: getting your product into the market.

The Rapid Learning Cycles Framework Supports Your Investors

Entrepreneurs go through a different set of phases than corporate R&D projects do, because corporate R&D projects get funded out of the R&D budget. Someone owns that budget, and normally there is a process for getting your project in the budget. Once you are in the budget, that owner expects to hear regularly about your progress. As long as the project meets expectations, it will probably continue to be funded until it's finished. The budget comes along with the need to be aligned with the company's overall strategy and standards. to deliver a product that does not harm the company's reputation in the market, and sometimes the requirement to leverage specific platform technologies.

Entrepreneurs don't have all the restrictions, but they still have to find the money. Even if all you need is a single injection mold, someone will need to write the check for it. Unless you are independently wealthy or your product is inexpensive to develop, you need to go through a funding phase to find investors and convince them that your vision and experience are worth their investment. You may need to go through more than one round of this before the product produces enough revenue to support the company you've built. Your relationship with these investors is an important piece to manage, and some types of investors require more management than others.

The great thing about the Rapid Learning Cycles framework in this context is that it provides you with the visibility you need to meet your investors' need to see progress, and gives them ways to get engaged if they want to be, without burdening you or the team with their demands.

If they want high visibility, you can share Key Decision Reports and Knowledge Gap Reports. You can invite them to see your Learning Cycles Plan. You can invite them to Learning Cycle and/or Integration Events, or you can hold investor updates right after these meetings, when the project is the clearest to you. You can give them as much as they truly need, and as much as you are willing to give—or as little. Since you will have a better grasp of the program, you will be better positioned to avoid surprising them with unpleasant news.

Rapid Learning Cycles Make Entrepreneurship More Fun and Less Frustrating

There is nothing more frustrating than getting stuck with a product that is 90% ready for launch - except for the problems that keep cropping up. It's a lot more fun to see customers pay for the privilege of using your product.

The Rapid Learning Cycles framework is all about keeping the program moving until you have that experience. As an entrepreneur, you may not have the time, money or patience to handle major project resets that could have been prevented. It's far better to conserve your cash so that you have the resources to adapt once you have the MVP in users' hands.

Learning cycles illuminate the path between the MVP and the product that fully realizes your vision. The product roadmap is a Key Decision to make relatively early and then update often. It may seem silly to have a roadmap for a product that doesn't even exist. But the whole point of an MVP is to evolve it rapidly. Roadmaps help you map out the product's increasing value as you enhance and refine it. You don't need to plan that far ahead—the next six months or even the next six weeks might be far enough.

The Learning Cycles Plan helps your team understand what's coming so that they can make decisions accordingly. You don't want to introduce one feature in such a way that it blocks another feature that is in the pipeline. If something turns out to be easier than expected, you may choose to accelerate it. It's easier to spot opportunities like this if there is a plan even if that plan is constantly changing.

CHAPTER FOURTEEN

Rapid Learning Cycles Across Product Development

The default Rapid Learning Cycles framework presented in this book was developed and evolved within Engineering and R&D teams. It is optimized for large programs to develop major new platforms or products that have priority within the organization and a desired launch date. The biggest challenge of implementing the default method is to change the mindset from doing to learning.

As soon as we started seeing successes with the method inside a company, other kinds of teams wanted to get on board. Some individuals saw conference presentations about the framework or a public workshop on Rapid Learning Cycles and decided that this method could help them, even though they were working on different types of programs.

Here are three variants that have been used to solve three specific challenges in corporate R&D.

The Rapid Learning Cycles Framework for Large, Complex Teams

The largest team I've ever helped to establish a Rapid Learning Cycles framework had over a dozen subteams, with critical business and technical hurdles to overcome. The program team set out to develop an entirely new technology that could revolutionize its industry, if it worked. The list of "known unknowns" filled an entire conference room wall with sticky notes, and the team had a deep pool of "unknown unknowns" that could emerge at any time. The team members needed the Rapid Learning Cycles framework to help them manage all of this uncertainty.

Large teams do have special needs. It's not feasible to get 150 people in a Status Event every week and people can spend too much time listening to things that don't affect them. Learning Cycle and Integration Events have to be tightly focused so that everyone can be heard. Here are the adaptations to meet the needs of a large team:

- **Kickoff Events with the entire group.** Even with a large team, everyone should participate in the Kickoff Event. Kickoff Events establish alignment around the Core Hypothesis and the general plan. It's helpful for everyone to hear about these things directly from you. Then they'll spend most of their time in their subteam, but you will be able to keep the subteams in sync with each other.

  They'll see the most important Key Decisions and Knowledge Gaps that other subteams have to close. When questions come up about the framework itself, you can give the same answer to everyone at once.

  When I kick off a team this large, the group spends about one-fourth of its time working together on alignment and integration, and three-fourths of its time in subteams, each focused on its own Key Decisions and Knowledge Gaps.

- **One common set of Key Decisions and Knowledge Gaps, with one Visual Plan.** We also see better results when the teams maintain one single list of Key Decisions and Knowledge Gaps with one Visual Plan to manage them all.

You and your subteam leaders need to see the big picture—all the things that all the subteams are working on. You need to be able to spot trouble areas that may occur across subteams. The subteams may—and probably should—maintain Activity Plans to manage their own work, which is the focus of Status Events.

- **Status Events by subteam, followed by team Status Events to coordinate team needs.** Since Status Events are focused on activities, they work best in subteams. The subteam Status Events feed into a smaller team Status Event attended only by subteam leaders.

    The leaders first understand how their own team is doing and then feed that information up. They listen for potential areas of conflict and opportunities to help across subteam boundaries. If there is any news to report back to their subteams, the leaders get it to the right people.

- **Learning Cycle Events with the whole group, subteam leaders or a combination.** Some program teams require all team members to participate in Learning Cycle Events. That is my default recommendation for the first few events with a team that is new to the methodology. It avoids inconsistencies in how team members approach their Knowledge Gap Reports and makes it easier to reinforce the shift from learning to doing.

    But it may not make sense for very long, if the subteams are working on areas that have little overlap. At some point, you may want to invite everyone but require only the subteam leaders to participate in the entire event. Everyone else can come and go. In all cases, the person who was responsible for closing the Knowledge Gap is the one who presents the Knowledge Gap Report—not the subteam leader.

- **Integration Events pull the whole team together for at least part of the event.** Integration Events are for everyone, even in very large teams. This is where Key Decisions get made and stakeholder feedback gets aired. As with Learning Cycle Events, it's OK for individuals to come and go.

  But if you have a room that's large enough, everyone should be invited to stay for the entire event, listening for potential conflicts and opportunities. It's a small amount of time to invest so that program integration goes smoothly. Usually, the meetings are engaging enough that you will have the opposite problem: too many people—especially unrelated managers—want to come!

Here are three mistakes to avoid when scaling the process up:

- **Failing to keep the group in sync as they learn the framework.** If the group is not kept close, you will end up with conflicting interpretations of key concepts like the Last Responsible Moment or the scope of a Knowledge Gap. You will need to work closely with your subteam leaders to ensure that there is consistency in between Learning Cycle and Integration Events.

- **Making subteam leaders responsible for all of their team's reports.** In traditional product development, a subteam leader would often take responsibility for delivering all of his or her team updates in the big meetings. But the shift from doing to learning is reinforced when the person who did the learning is the one who reports and makes the recommendation. Young team members or lab technicians are often assigned to run experiments and collect observations. Consider including their firsthand experience when it's time for the reports, even if they are not the Knowledge Gap owners.

- **Trying to attend every event yourself.** You don't need to attend every subteam Status Event after the first set. Your time is better spent building stakeholder relationships and working with subteam leaders to maintain alignment and reinforce the vision you have for your product.

Large programs normally consume a lot of project management overhead and carry high risks that the cost and consequences of late changes will overwhelm the organization with unexpected work and expenses. Rapid Learning Cycles help cut through the complexity to focus everyone on the things that are the most important to address early.

The Rapid Learning Cycles Framework for Advanced Research Labs

The Rapid Learning Cycles framework has worked very well for structuring experimentation in advanced research labs that seek to push the limits of technology without the need for immediate commercialization. This is an environment where the failure rate is high and the urgency is low. When the lab does come up with something that can be commercialized, it is still years away from being a product.

In this environment, Rapid Learning Cycles provide a lightweight, agile program framework, visibility and urgency. The team may already organize its work into major research programs and then define Key Decisions (the overall research strategy) and Knowledge Gaps (the hypotheses to test). Or it may define Key Decisions and Knowledge Gaps as a department or lab, with lots of different small investigations going on at once.

Sometimes people working in this environment get isolated from each other, since their work doesn't naturally overlap. The Rapid Learning Cycles framework can make their work more visible to one another, so that it's easier to identify areas of synergy and opportunities to help each other. They often find that the Learning Cycle and Integration Events are engaging, rich discussions where they get good peer feedback and the opportunity to learn about new areas of research.

It takes one group Kickoff Event to get started and then the process can run continuously. It helps if this Kickoff Event coincides with the process for determining the group's research priorities for the year. It might be helpful to have one preliminary Kickoff Event prior to the lab's research portfolio review, to see what Key Decisions and Knowledge Gaps people are working toward, and then to hold a second one after the portfolio is established for the next year. After that, a little bit of replanning at the Integration Events should keep the Learning Cycles Plan current.

Since this is exploratory work, some groups prefer to use the concept of Critical Questions instead of Key Decisions. Critical Questions are like big Knowledge Gaps that the team would like to close: "How does the body's immune system respond when it encounters a cancer cell for the first time?" Researchers have been trying to answer this question with many different experimental approaches for a long time. The main Critical Question serves the same coordination function as the Core Hypothesis does for a product team: it reminds the team of the long-term goals of the research program.

Research groups can break these large questions down into smaller Critical Questions (or Knowledge Gaps): "Does the human T-cell leukemia virus affect signaling by INF-alpha?" The team can organize the smaller questions into a logical sequence, just as the program team puts its Key Decisions into sequence.

Although these Critical Questions may not have Last Responsible Moments, it's still helpful for the team to hold periodic reviews with stakeholders to assess the progress it is making. Otherwise, it risks becoming invisible to the rest of the organization.

The Status Events happen less frequently—no more than weekly but no less than every two weeks—but the structure remains the same. The Learning Cycle Events can be monthly, every two months or quarterly. They become the lab's opportunity to share their work with one another.

The presentations focus on the experiments that have been running, new experimental methods that have been developed or new lines of research that have emerged from monitoring the literature or attending conferences. The Integration Events are the teams' opportunity to make their work visible to a larger group, including the people who determine the budgets for the labs. There may not be much "integration" if the teams are working on small projects, but you will see rich discussion about possible synergies.

The Rapid Learning Cycles Framework for Incremental Product Development

On the opposite end of the spectrum are those programs that are supposed to run quickly: extend a technology into a new market with little change or make an incremental improvement while keeping most of it the same. Too often these programs turn out to be a lot harder than they look on the surface, or they encounter a lot of "scope creep" as stakeholders add new requirements to the product. The Rapid Learning Cycles framework helps these teams ensure that the development phase is as small as it seems to be, and stays that way.

These programs still need an Evaluation Phase to understand the need for the product and to scope out any major Key Decisions and Knowledge Gaps. This phase can go quickly—it can be as short as a single learning cycle. The purpose of this phase is to validate the group's assumption that this program will be fast—that the gap between the current product and the new one is small and easily closed. Once this gap has been defined, it will be easier to say no to a stakeholder who wants to make it bigger.

The team then needs a Learning Phase. The length of this phase should be set after the Evaluation Phase, when the team knows a little more about the gap between the current product and the new one. The Learning Phase can be as short as one additional learning cycle if there are no Key Decisions and just a few Knowledge Gaps. The evaluation team may also learn that this is not incremental development. That will fundamentally alter and may destroy the business case for the product, but it is far better to know that before the group starts major work.

The structure is otherwise the same, although the team may be able to maintain a faster cadence because it can leverage a lot of knowledge from the existing product.

The Rapid Learning Cycles Framework for Customized Product Development

If you are in a market where you develop custom products from standard platforms, you need two Rapid Learning Cycles framework variants:

- **Platform Development.** This framework variant is used for the major technology updates that keep your product offerings competitive and deliver major new customer benefits. This type of development program builds extensible knowledge, and the main challenge is to encapsulate that knowledge effectively so that the custom programs don't have much work to do.

- **Custom Development.** This is the work to develop products that meet the needs of specific customers. The main challenges of this type of program are the need to balance customer needs and desires against the platform's capabilities, avoid overpromising and manage scope continuously until the program is finished.

Both of these variants use the core framework elements: Key Decisions, Knowledge Gaps and all of the events.

A platform is a bundle of extensible knowledge, encapsulated in reusable subsystems, components, design patterns/templates and foundational knowledge. The Knowledge Gap and Key Decision reports capture the foundational knowledge that helps the Customization Teams use platform technology more effectively.

The Platform Development framework is the default framework I have described in Section Four, with an extra emphasis on capturing knowledge for later reuse. If you have to customize products, it's especially important to have visual models that describe the system's performance, so that you can tune each product variant to meet the specific customer request. You need to know if your customer is asking for something that exceeds the limits of the existing platform.

The Custom Development framework looks like the Incremental Development framework from the previous section, as long as customers want to do things that the platform can already do. The Evaluation Phase of the program will help you identify the options to present to customers, and the Key Decisions and Knowledge Gaps you need to close. Some groups even invite customers to participate in the events to identify Key Decisions and Knowledge Gaps so that they can make better-informed decisions themselves.

Since many customers want their products yesterday, you will face temptation and pressure to compress the Learning Phase or remove it altogether. Yet your ability to deliver on your promises to your customers depends upon the effectiveness of this phase. If something is not going to work as expected, the customer is better off knowing it early, when there is still time to pursue other alternatives. If schedule performance is important to the relationship, the Learning Phase will help you avoid the loopbacks that delay delivery.

Customers who are paying you for development naturally want to receive updates on your progress. The Learning Cycles Plan will help you make these updates more meaningful to them. You may be able to convince them that they can learn enough by participating in Integration Events or in meetings that immediately follow these events, without elaborate status updates that take your time away from the thing they care about most: their product.

Programs That Are Not Good Fits for the Framework

There are a few types of programs for which the Rapid Learning Cycles framework does not work well, primarily because the assumptions underlying this method do not match the program, or because other, simpler methods suffice. For others, Rapid Learning Cycles have some usefulness at the subsystem level, but the overall system requires a different approach. These include:

- Pure software or service development for a known customer who is engaged, including internal IT, web and app development. Agile Software Development is tailored for these programs. If there are no major Key Decisions with significant Knowledge Gaps, the project is primarily execution driven and the structures of Agile Development will suffice.

- Design-focused products made using existing technology, such as traditional furniture, clothing and dinnerware. In these product categories, the artistry of the designer predominates, while the underlying technology may not have changed for centuries.

  There are exceptions to this rule: an outdoor clothing company may choose to run Rapid Learning Cycles on new product concepts that require the use of new materials or garment construction methods. The question to ask is, "How new is the process and/or the materials required to produce the finished product? How different is it at the foundation level from other products of its type?"

- Very large programs, such as new car platforms, airplanes and new defense systems. These programs, with thousands of engineers working on multiple subsystems simultaneously, require a higher level of coordination than the Rapid Learning Cycles framework provides.

  They have formal, heavyweight PDPs because such large projects require formal structured communication. Individual groups can run Rapid Learning Cycles for the portion of the program allotted to feasibility studies, and may continue to run them to eliminate risks. Suppliers to these industries see tremendous benefit from the Customized Product variant of the framework. They can also run Rapid Learning Cycles on incremental products for which the degree of change requires a much smaller team.

Pharma and some medical devices are hybrids. Rapid Learning Cycles work well alongside the structured processes required to get regulatory approval until clinical testing, when the standard procedural PDP takes over. The early learning cycles flush out issues that would otherwise stay hidden before the product reaches the most expensive part of the development process.

The sweet spot for this method is a program team of at least 3 but no more than 150 on a single program, organized as a single team or as one layer of subteams, working on a program that would typically take from a year to five years. We see benefits from using the framework on a program like this even if it's not completely implemented or there were problems with executing the framework.

How to Start the Rapid Learning Cycles Framework If You Have Already Started Your Program

If you picked up this book because you have a product that is in development and you want to get it to market as fast as possible, you can start the Rapid Learning Cycles framework wherever you are. However, you have probably accumulated some "knowledge debt" in the form of Key Decisions that you made without the knowledge to make them, or even the analysis to see what you needed to know in order to make them stick.

When I encounter a team like this, we do a Kickoff Event as if it was a new program. We look for upcoming Key Decisions, sequence them and break them down into Knowledge Gaps. Then we take some time to reflect on the program's history: what Key Decisions have been made already, and how risky were those decisions? It's easier to see the past Key Decisions after the team has gained experience by looking ahead. We break these decisions down into their Knowledge Gaps, to make the knowledge debt more visible.

When we prioritize, we include the Knowledge Gaps that were not closed earlier. Depending upon the program, it may be worth investing some time to close them now, so that if a Key Decision needs to be corrected, we can do it sooner when it is easier. Or it could be that the team decides to focus on making its upcoming Key Decisions with as much knowledge as possible. The final answer is usually a blend of the past and future.

Finally, we establish the cadences and events, then build the Learning Cycles Plan. If you are already into Detailed Design, you will need to integrate this with your overall project plan, allocating some resources for closing Knowledge Gaps. You can take out some of the time in the program you have set aside for loopbacks, if your organization supports that. If products usually launch late, you probably won't launch as late as the typical program, but there is still likely to be a major loopback or two.

Rarely, there is so much knowledge debt that the team needs to take a time-out from doing in order to learn. If this is the case, you need to get your sponsor and stakeholders on board with a plan to temporarily halt development now to avoid a major project reset close to launch. It's more likely that your program needs attention in a few focused areas to reduce risk. You will not see the time-to-market improvements that you would have seen if you had used the framework from the beginning, because you are likely to run into issues that cause loopbacks. But if you can prevent the worst of them, the product launch should go more smoothly than it would have if you had not adopted the framework.

Even if the team does not choose to take any time to learn about past Knowledge Gaps to reduce its debt, it is still better off because it can see the risks it has taken. This makes it easier to notice when things are not working out as expected, so that fewer issues become crises at the end.

CHAPTER FIFTEEN

Tracking Rapid Learning Cycle Progress

I can tell when a Rapid Learning Cycles program is going well. The team is engaged. The events are dynamic. The Program Leader knows how much to expect from the team, when to push a little and when to back off. The Knowledge Gap and Key Decision reports are clear, even to me as an outsider.

When your team is working well, you will know. But if something needs adjustment, it will be easier to spot if you have been observing the team, reflecting on the results and monitoring some carefully selected metrics.

Things to Observe

I'll start with what to notice about the framework itself. When you are attending team meetings or walking around your office, these are some things to look for to give you a sense of the overall program. They are not quantitative metrics, but they are leading indicators of the results that will show up in the program metrics if you are not paying attention. It's easier to make adjustments when the team is new and the program is not very far along than it will be to make them later, after team norms have crystallized and the program is in its busiest phases.

- **How is the team's general morale and stress level?** Are people relaxed and calm, or are they a little frantic? Do they seem to be overloaded? How much tension is in the office? Do people seem to be working well as a team?

- **What happens at Status Events?** Are there a lot of activities that need help? Is the group able to keep the meetings short and efficient? Are the team members beginning to hold themselves accountable for following good Status Event practices?

- **What happens at Learning Cycle and Integration Events?** Are Knowledge Gaps closing? Are Key Decisions being made? Do the team members actively participate in the discussion, or do they mostly listen passively? Do the reports share conclusions and recommendations or just data and information?

- **How well written are the Knowledge Gap and Key Decision Reports?** Do they capture what you need to know now? Do they capture what you will need to know for the next version of the product, so that you don't have to do the experiments over again? Do they contain links to the important backup information?

- **What do you hear from the stakeholders?** Are they engaged? How much visibility does this program have outside the team? Does this program seem to have the priority that it merits?

- **What do you hear from the team?** What do the team members say about the process when you speak to them one on one? Are they getting used to it? Do they like it? If not, why? What are the sources of friction for them?

- **How engaged are customers helping you with Early Look Feedback Sessions?** If you have customers engaged to help you close Knowledge Gaps, how responsive are they? How effective are your methods for working with them? How good is the information you're getting from your work together?

- **What do you observe?** What do you notice about yourself? What are the sources of friction for you? Has the method helped you become a better leader, coach and partner, or is it making things harder for you? How worried are you about the team and the product right now? Does it seem as though the team is building the product you have envisioned? If not, why not?

Take these observations back to the team, in a brief reflection at the end of the Learning Cycle Event. Ask them to take some time to discuss the framework: what's working, what's not working and what adjustments they would like to make. Even fifteen minutes spent on a short Reflection Event will help the team identify and eliminate sources of friction, so they can focus more on the product itself. Make changes outside of the Learning Cycle Event only if something is obviously not working and has become a major source of pain and frustration. It's more important to maintain the framework's stability between the events than it is to continually optimize.

Metrics for Monitoring the Rapid Learning Cycles Program

David Packard, one of HP's founders, often said, "What gets measured gets done." If you don't know where you are, how will you know that you have changed for the better? What does success look like?

Even if you sense that your program is going well, you need to prove that to others, especially the sponsor who is supporting you and the other stakeholders whom you depend upon to get the product out the door. You need to demonstrate that the Rapid Learning Cycles framework is an improvement over traditional product development as practiced at your company. You may need to prove to investors that this framework is leading to the product you have promised to deliver.

Product Metrics vs. Process Metrics vs. Results Metrics

You are considering Rapid Learning Cycles because you want something specific: the shortest path between you and your new product. If it's important to you or to your company, you can define metrics around that result, and around other desirable outcomes like better quality or lower costs. These results metrics are important for determining whether the Rapid Learning Cycles framework has delivered its promised value. But the time it takes to show these results diminishes their power to have any impact on the results.

You also need to demonstrate that you have delivered a great product. That the product is not too expensive to make and does not drain away money on warranty repairs and support calls. That the product sells well and provides the company with a nice profit from each sale. You can establish some metrics that predict the product's performance. These metrics give you the visibility you need to make adjustments so that the product will be more likely to hit your targets. In fact, for something like Cost of Goods Sold (COGS), you're almost certain to miss the mark if you don't monitor it early and often.

We use process metrics to help us understand the health of the program while the program is running. They generate stronger pull for good results because they are more immediate. Process metrics measure one piece of the overall program in order to predict the outcome of the whole. They can be dangerous because the whole does not equal the sum of its parts. A lot of program teams hit their dates for the first three phases of their PDP and then struggle with loopbacks in the last stage before development. As long as you are able to remember that predictions of success are just predictions, process metrics can help you spot problems quickly.

When reporting a program's results metrics, it's best to create a bridge between the short-term process metrics and their long-term counterparts, and then report them both together. This is especially true if you are trying a new method like the Rapid Learning Cycles framework and want to demonstrate the contribution that the new method has made to your program's success. The combination is especially powerful because the senior leaders see that they are getting what they want, and the people on the team see the connection to the things they did differently to achieve the results. There are few better ways to ensure that your sponsors and team will be eager to use the Rapid Learning Cycles framework again.

How to Define a Metric

A metric is an answer to the question, "How will we know that we have succeeded?" The short-term answers become your process metrics, while the long-term answers lead toward results metrics. Ideally, it's not too difficult to gather the underlying data or calculate the metric, and the methodology makes sense to everyone.

A good metric begins with good definitions for its key terms that don't conflict with other organizational meanings. What does it mean to be done? How do you know that a Knowledge Gap has been closed? How do you define the Integration Event? How does your Finance department calculate COGS?

A good metric is measurable. Some things, like team engagement, are subjective and therefore hard to quantify. You may have to find a proxy, such as the number of people who participate in team celebrations. You may need to use an employee satisfaction survey.

A good metric is actionable. There is a clear link between the metric and the things people can do to change the metric.

Finally, you need to know how you are going to collect this data. You rarely have existing data to support process metrics. You will need to develop the mechanism and timing for collecting results. The metrics will be believed only if people understand how you collected the data and what methods you used to analyze it.

The Balanced Scorecard for the Innovation Program

Some groups establish a long list of metrics, but this just adds a lot of work for you as the Program Leader, without adding much value to the program. You need to be selective about the metrics you monitor. If you are in a process-heavy organization that measures everything, you will need to prioritize the metrics you track even more.

I recommend that innovation teams use a modified Balanced Scorecard approach to metrics. As described by Robert Kaplan, Balanced Scorecards have Financial, Customer, Operations and Learning & Growth metrics. The scorecard in Figure 13.1 splits Operations into Product Health and Process Health. I replace Learning & Growth with Team Health, because team members learn and grow a lot by virtue of participating in a Rapid Learning Cycles program. Team members' participation in corporate training experiences should be tracked elsewhere.

- **Financial.** The projected and actual financial performance of the product. Process metrics should show that the product is forecast to sell at a profitable price to achieve a good Return on Investment (ROI). This requires modeling price performance, which depends on the business model, feature set and competitive offerings. COGS models work best when you establish a cost budget with guidelines and an escalation path for exceeding it.

- **Customer.** The projected and actual customer engagement for the product. Process metrics measure the amount and effectiveness of customer engagement during development, before there is a product to buy. The results metrics capture the number of customers vs. the forecast number, but also their reactions to the product as measured by reviews and customer ratings.

- **Product Health.** The projected and actual quality of the product. The time taken to close technical Key Decisions is a leading indicator: if decisions get taken late too often, there could be problems with the system architecture or the general approach. The other process metrics measure product quality and how quickly the team is able to resolve issues. The results metrics all reflect the cost or impact of design flaws.

- **Process Health.** The current state and impact of the Rapid Learning Cycles framework. Process metrics help you monitor the health of the framework. Results metrics help you demonstrate that the framework made a difference.

- **Team Health.** The current state of team engagement, and the impact on team members after the program is finished. The process metrics in this area help you spot problems within your team before they affect the program. The results metrics gauge your team members' reaction to the framework after they have been through one complete program.

In the table, I give two or three sample metrics in each category. Please don't try to keep track of them all. If you choose one from each row, you will have five process metrics and five results metrics, a reasonable number to collect without too much impact on your time.

	Process	Results
Financial	COGS Model	ROI vs Forecast
	Projected ROI	COGS vs Forecast
	Projected Pricing Model	Time to Breakeven
Customer	Customer Key Decisions Made on Time	Unit Sales vs. Forecast
	Customer Validation Test Results	Conversion Rates
	Beta Test / Early Look Program Participation	Reviews and Customer Ratings

	Process	Results
Product Health	Technical Key Decisions Made on Time Product Validation Test Results Curves Number of High Priority Knowledge Gaps Closed Prior to the Related Key Decision	Support and Warranty Costs Scrap and Defect Rates Product Return Rate
Process Health	Key Decisions Made on Time Percentage of High Priority Knowledge Gaps Closed Length of Status Meetings	Number and Impact of Loopbacks vs. Similar Products Projected vs. Actual Launch Date Time Spent in Industrialization vs. Similar Products
Team Health	Invitees vs. Attendees at Integration Events Timeliness and Accuracy of Knowledge Gap and Key Decision Reports Employee Turnover or Reassignments During the Program	Team Satisfaction Survey Requests to Use the Framework Again Employee Turnover in the Quarter After Launch

These metrics are only suggestions. It will be better if you ask the question, "How will we know that the program is going well?" and then use these examples to formulate your own metrics, using the words that are most meaningful to your team and stakeholders.

Metrics to Monitor Your Product Roadmap with a Cadenced

Release Plan

The metrics just described all assume a development program that is aimed toward a single product launch. What if your plan is to release a series of products into the market, starting with an MVP, so that you can learn from real customers and then adjust? You would follow a cadenced release strategy so that customers won't need to wait for the perfect solution to begin getting value from our product, and because there are things you need to know about the product that you cannot learn any other way. The Core Hypothesis is not completely proven until paying customers have validated it. For this strategy to succeed, you need to choose your metrics carefully to maximize the learning you get from each release cycle.

I call this model a "cadenced release" strategy because it flows best for you and for your customers if there is a regular rhythm to the releases. That way, the release plan gains all the benefits of cadence that a team experiences with learning cycles: the ability to coordinate work with each other by aligning work with the program's heartbeat. In practice, I would align most product releases with Learning Cycle or Integration Events and use the event either to finalize the contents of the new release or to review the release after it has been live to determine where to go next. The main objective is to establish and sustain a regular schedule. You, your support teams and your customers will benefit from a regular rhythm that will make the series of releases seem orderly and manageable instead of chaotic and disorganized.

You can choose to release very often—weekly or even daily if this is a web application with no client software at all. If clients have to download software or update apps, they may get annoyed if the updates are too frequent. You can choose to conduct a Learning Cycle Event after every two or three releases, instead of every time. You can choose to release a new product after quarterly Integration Events, or even annually for a complex product. I advise groups that are launching a major platform development program to consider ways to break the platform release down into a series of smaller releases so that customers don't have to wait three years to start benefiting from the team's work.

You need the same categories of metrics, because your overall strategy is at risk if you are burning out team members or the Rapid Learning Cycles framework is decaying in the heat of the launch release series. You will monitor Product Health, Process Health and Team Health throughout to ensure that the stress of the product release cycle is not causing instability in the product quality, the Rapid Learning Cycles framework or team dynamics.

But you will watch the Financial and Customer metrics most closely to differentiate between different versions of the product. The metrics that you track in those areas will be structured a little differently to highlight the differences between the releases.

- **Release-specific metrics to test hypotheses.** A cadenced release is a learning cycle, even if there is more than one of them between Learning Cycle Events. You can release a series of products based upon a feature set that you have predefined, so that each version of the product is better than the last one. That fulfills the first objective of cadenced releases. But it's better to structure your releases to close those Knowledge Gaps you can't close without real customer data. The shift from doing to learning doesn't end just because the first product has been released. A cadenced release strategy requires you to treat every release like the experiment it is:

  - Observations: What are your observations about current customer response? What would you like to change?

  - Hypothesis: Why are customers doing something different than what we want them to do? How have others made it easier for customers to take the next step?

  - Experimental design: The product with the updates that you expect to improve customer response.

- Run: Release the product, and measure the specific behavior that you expect to change from your updates.
- Capture knowledge: What happened? How did that match your prediction in your hypothesis?

- **Product variant metrics to support Convergence.** With this type of test, you extend the concept of convergence after the product launch. Rather than releasing a single product, you release a set of product variants to see how they perform with customers. This type of test is easier to do in software, but it is not impossible to do in hardware if you use modular design and rapid prototyping technology to produce limited editions that can go out to early-look customers.

  Google popularized the use of split testing, presenting some changes only to selected users based on user data and using other means to experiment on users for Internet applications. If your product is modular, with interface elements that are easy to change, you can apply the same techniques to other types of software or to physical products: what happens when early-look users receive a product with the keypad on the left vs. in the middle?

- **Cohort metrics to measure customer engagement improvements.** If customers have been exposed to different product variants, then they differ from one another based on the product they saw first, even if they have all received the same updates. Cohort analysis breaks your customer metrics down by product release, so that you can keep track of how your changes have affected customer behavior over time. Each customer group that encountered your product during a specific product release is measured together in a cohort of all the customers that first experienced that product release.

  For example, you may have experienced a lot of misuse of the product in early versions because the interface was confusing or the industrial design led customers to make the wrong assumptions about how to use it. Even if you give those early customers new products that fix the problem, they have still learned the "wrong" way to use the product and will react differently than a later group that has used product correctly from the beginning.

Cadenced releases support cohort metrics because it is easy to match customers to product variants. That will give you greater visibility into the impact of the changes you made in each variant. If you release continually or on an irregular schedule, it will be difficult to group customers into meaningful cohorts.

Metrics That Waste Your Time

Some metrics simply aren't worth tracking, even though they might seem like a good idea. Either they either measure things that are not measurable, or the measures encourage teams to do the wrong things instead of the right ones. Avoid the temptation to establish measures like these:

- **Number of Knowledge Gaps closed or the time it takes to close them.** Knowledge Gaps vary so much in size and importance that it's not worthwhile to count them. Some groups have experimented with using Story Points (a tool from Agile Software Development) to estimate the duration of a Knowledge Gap. The Story Points were designed for use on User Stories that require software development. Usually, the number of points is determined by the amount of design work that needs to be done. But since the technology is known, the work is predictable. Knowledge Gaps don't work like that—if they did, we wouldn't need to close them.

- **Schedule variance.** The activity schedule changes so often, and there is so little visibility into what needs to be done at the beginning, that measuring schedule variance at the activity level is useless. Even the Learning Cycles Plan is too dynamic. If you have to measure conformance to plan, measure it at the level of Key Decisions. Those are the elements that get on the critical path if they are not made on time.

- **Time or money required to reach individual gates.** Measuring how rapidly a group takes to get to Detailed Design encourages them to take shortcuts in the Learning Phases—and that is exactly what they should not be doing. Using Rapid Learning Cycles will require more time in the early phases but you will make up that time in late development.

- **Percentage completion of anything.** Activities are done or not done. Knowledge Gaps are closed or open. Key Decisions have been made or have not been made. Major milestones are reached on time or not. Too many projects get stuck in "90 percent complete" for more than a quarter of the total schedule for "percentage completion" to be a useful metric.

- **Growth metrics.** Growth metrics, such as unit sales increases, don't tell you very much because there is no link between the growth number and the things you did or didn't do that would foster or inhibit growth. The data is easy to collect, but it's too difficult to interpret in an actionable way. For a single product, all you can measure is your performance against another similar product, or the incremental addition to revenue from new customers. Growth metrics may help you evaluate the company's overall product strategy, but they don't help the program nearly as much as measuring actual vs. forecasted revenue and adoption curves. For a startup, paying too much attention to these metrics can be deadly: you don't know where the growth or lack of it is coming from without more relevant information on customer behavior.

Although the ultimate measures of your success are relentlessly objective—revenue, cost, quality and market acceptance—the best measures to use to run your program don't require a calculator. They mainly require you to use your powers of observation.

What Do You See?

All of these metrics don't replace your own two eyes and ears. What do you see and hear? What observations do you have? What's not as smooth as you'd like it to be? What's working better than you expected?

Observations

When I visit a client site, I like to walk through the team workspaces and visit their conference rooms. I'm usually not looking for anything specific. I just visit the spaces as quietly as I can, and ask myself what I notice:

- What's on the walls or in the conference rooms? Are they using visual models to communicate, or a lot of text and numbers? Do IT and Legal policies get in the way of their ability to share information? (If the walls are bare, that's usually why.) Does it look like they inhabit the space, or is it a bit sterile? Does the space support collaboration and creativity?

- What are people doing when they're not in an event? Are they at their desks working alone? Are they working in pairs? Are there a lot of impromptu meetings in conference rooms or the coffee area? Is it a noisy or quiet space? (Either is OK, just different.) Does the room seem energized or tired?

- What time do people come in, and when do they leave? Relative to the company norms, are people eager to get to work? Do they stay late? Do they perhaps stay later than they should or work weekends? Where do they take lunches or breaks?

- How easy is it for non-collocated team members to participate fully in the program? Is the audio or video quality OK for remote meetings? Does the team manage time zone differences well so that team members don't have to disrupt their sleep? Are the key elements of the Rapid Learning Cycles framework—the logs and Learning Cycles Plan—available online for remote teams to view? Has the team had a face-to-face with their remote colleagues?

- What keeps you up at night? Finally, what are you most worried about right now? I knew we were on to something special with the Rapid Learning Cycles framework when one of our early adopters told me that she was completely relaxed over the Christmas break—the program was on track and she had nothing to worry about. If you are not in that space, why not?

Reflection Events to Tailor the Framework

It takes a few cycles to learn how to use this framework. Achieving mastery is partly a function of being willing to do what the framework tells you to do, even if it's counter-intuitive. Another part of mastery is knowing when to adapt the framework to meet the needs of your specific program. How do you tell the difference?

Reflection Events create an opportunity for you and the team to master the framework together by exposing the things that are working well and the things that need to be adjusted. When team members see that their concerns get addressed and that friction gets removed, they can relax.

This does not need to take a long time. A half hour at the end of a Learning Cycle Event or an Integration Event is enough to get the team's answers to these questions:

- What is going well?
- What do we need to adjust?
- What should we stop doing?
- What changes should we consider?

After the first learning cycle, the team may want to change a lot of things—and some of those things may be in direct contradiction to the fundamental principles of the framework. If they want to go back to traditional project management where they feel more comfortable, your answer has to be no.

I also recommend that inexperienced teams run the Rapid Learning Cycles framework as tightly as possible without a lot of changes. It's easier to see what changes you need once the team has firsthand experience with the default framework.

Other things will be more clear. I've mentioned that you have the freedom to set your own cadence, and to adjust the cadence as long as you don't adjust it too often. You can make improvements to the Knowledge Gap or Key Decision templates, or where they get posted. You can make adjustments to the Learning Cycles Planning Board to get it to work better for you.

Then you have the adjustments that are in the gray zone. If you are unsure as to whether to make a change, I recommend rereading the first two chapters to refresh yourself on the primary purpose of Rapid Learning Cycles: to eliminate long learning cycles that cause program delays. Then reflect on the principles that are embedded in the framework:

- Set a regular cadence.
- Push decisions later and pull learning forward.
- Identify and validate your Core Hypothesis.
- Capture the things that you learn in extensible form.
- Make the program's plans more visible.

- Use a consistent investigation process that's grounded in the Scientific Method.
- Never stop driving the vision.

The right decision will be the one that pulls you closer to these principles, even if it seems uncomfortable or counter-intuitive.

We typically hold Reflection Events after the first three Learning Cycle Events, and after the first two Integration Events, and then hold them at least once every six months after that until the program has concluded. Experienced teams can skip some of the early ones, but still need a regular reflection twice per year to ensure that the framework does not degrade.

Chances are, some things are going well and other things need adjustment. The next chapter will show you how.

CHAPTER SIXTEEN

Options, Obstacles and Speed Bumps

A s with any method, there are things about the Rapid Learning Cycles framework that you need to follow closely so that the program runs smoothly. In other areas you have a lot of freedom to create your own way of working, to find just the right fit for your program and your team.

In this chapter, I'll describe some of the speed bumps that teams often run into as they use the framework for the first time. I'll discuss the major ones that can hurt the team and should be actively avoided, and then some minor ones that are easy to step over if you bump into them. I'll review the areas where there are a lot of right answers, including innovative solutions your team may develop. Then I'll end the chapter with the actions to take when it looks as though things are off track.

The Five Major Obstacles to Overcome

The Rapid Learning Cycles framework has a few known obstacles that cause teams to get stuck. The problems cause the team to either abandon the framework altogether or miss something important, triggering the type of late surprise that the framework is supposed to prevent.

Unproductive Events with Unclear Boundaries

Learning Cycle and Integration Events are designed to have strict boundaries between status updates, knowledge sharing and decision making. This is because we are comfortable with status updates. We're also comfortable making decisions—but not making data-driven decisions. We are not at all comfortable with knowledge sharing. Without boundaries, the knowledge sharing tends to get lost as teams naturally gravitate toward their comfort zones. This failure mode is especially destructive because it undermines the foundation of the Rapid Learning Cycles framework.

You will know that you are experiencing this failure mode if your Learning Cycle Events become status meetings where people share what they have done, instead of sharing what they have learned. They may describe an experiment in detail and present the data, but stop there. For the data they have generated to become knowledge, they need to have analyzed and interpreted it. They need to give their best recommendation, and they need to make the recommendation the focus of their communication—not the path they took to arrive at it.

We prevent this problem by recognizing that the shift from doing to learning is difficult, and then carving out protected space for the learning piece. We maintain good boundaries in the Learning Cycle Event by suppressing our own tendencies to ask status-related questions. As people learn to make this transition, we respectfully ask people to stop reporting status, instead asking them questions about the knowledge they've gained and their recommendations. We hold a Status Event before the Learning Cycle Event to provide a container for all the status updates that people feel they should give, so that they can focus their attention on learning during the main event.

The Wrong People or Too Many People at the Kickoff Event

As a consultant, I find that this one happens to me a lot, because when I come in to help the group's first Rapid Learning Cycles team, everyone else wants to take advantage of the training aspects of the Kickoff Event. We'll get other teams' Program Leaders and project managers, PDP Process Owners, and people who will join the team later.

But I've learned through painful experience that it's not helpful for the team to have a lot of extra people in the room. Since they are not familiar with the program, they tend to suggest Key Decisions and Knowledge Gaps that lead the team off track. One or two extra people are fine—in fact, if they can function as expert reviewers, their input can be quite valuable. But a subteam should not have more than one extra person in it when it is doing small group work during the Kickoff Event.

It's important that the team members—and not functional managers—participate in the Kickoff Event personally. Service group managers whose teams perform specific tasks, such as market studies or toxicology testing, may represent their teams. But if an engineering discipline's functional manager has already assigned people to support the Learning Phase of the program, the assigned individuals are the ones to have in the room—without their functional manager.

You will know that you had the wrong people or too many people if the team ends up with a lot of irrelevant Key Decisions and Knowledge Gaps to sort through after the Kickoff Event. The Learning Cycles Plan may be cluttered with things that the team already knows or that have lower priority. In fact, you may need to rerun the Kickoff Event quietly with just the team, in order to make sure they have chosen the right Key Decisions and Knowledge Gaps to focus on.

We prevent this problem by being careful with the guest list for Kickoff Events, restricting participation to those team members who have a key role to play in the next phase of the program, plus a few selected downstream functional representatives who need to be engaged early.

Manufacturing and test engineers, procurement agents and regulatory affairs can do a better job if they have the chance to identify their own Knowledge Gaps now, and if they have visibility into the team's Key Decision sequence. Other people, including extra managers, should be kept out of the room.

Failure to Maintain Learning Cycle Cadence

The learning cycle cadence is the heartbeat of the program, creating urgency and surfacing problems. It's important to set a cadence and stick to it, so that people can align their work to the rhythm of the program. If the learning cycle cadence does not get established, the team will never develop the sense of timing that pulls learning through the program.

Some team leaders have told me that they did not start seeing all the benefits of Rapid Learning Cycles until they tightened up their cadences. They were closing Knowledge Gaps and making Key Decisions, but the program kept getting bogged down because there was no pull or rhythm.

You will recognize this failure mode because it happens only if you allow it to happen, and you may be the one causing it. If you allow the Learning Cycle Events to get delayed for any reason, from an inconclusive experiment to an outbreak of the flu, you will throw off the rhythm of the team. The only exception to this rule is an officewide closure for the holidays or a trade show that is planned in advance.

Without a regular cadence, the team just sputters along and things don't get done. If it's OK to cancel or delay a Learning Cycle or Integration Event, they will get delayed—almost every time. This robs the team of the chance to surface the root causes of the delays. As the delays add up, pressure will mount to move into the next phase of development prematurely. The team will not learn what it needs to know to execute later phases without loopbacks. Those loopbacks will then delay the program even more.

It is OK to change the cadence if you do it with intention at a Learning Cycle Event, where the team has a chance to align with the new cycle length, and as long as you don't change the cadence more than once a quarter. The problems arise when you do not maintain any cadence at all, change it too often or allow events to get rescheduled.

Too Many Key Decisions and Knowledge Gaps

Sometimes teams can be overwhelmed by the sheer number of Key Decisions and Knowledge Gaps that they have in their Learning Cycles Plan. This creates an overload state, which forces individuals to prioritize their own work. If the team, with your guidance, does not establish strong priorities and commits to doing more than it can do, different people will choose to work on different things.

This is a common problem for a team's first attempt to use the Rapid Learning Cycles framework. It's difficult to know how long it will take to close Knowledge Gaps without some experience. The effect is that teams end up working on things that are not necessarily your priorities: they work on the interesting things or the easy things instead of the most important things. Their work is spread across too many Knowledge Gaps for too many Key Decisions. The Learning Cycles Plan begins to show a "snowplow" effect, in which things pile up in the first column of the plan because too many different things are in motion and nothing is getting driven to completion.

You can prevent this by keeping the team a little underloaded at the Kickoff Event, but in practice, that is hard because the team is eager to learn everything. In most programs, we monitor things carefully for the first few cycles and then revise the Learning Cycles Plan to bring it in line with the team's true capacity. Give the team ample time to review the plan and revise it at the first several Learning Cycle Events. The team needs your support to help it cut the number of prioritized Knowledge Gaps so that it can focus on the most important ones. Remember, the goal is not to achieve perfection—it is to achieve a major improvement. For most teams, that's enough to drive a substantial decrease in time to market. Chances are, you would not have taken the time to close any of these Knowledge Gaps if you had followed a traditional process.

No Deadline for the Learning Phases

The Learning Phases of the program need end dates. There will always be more to learn and risk can always be reduced further with one more study. But the desire to eliminate all risk is always balanced by the need to get the product into customers' hands.

If this phase doesn't have a clear end date, it goes on until someone, usually some high-level manager, gets impatient. What happens next depends upon how visible this program is to him or her. You could be told that you have to move to the next phase immediately, or the program may be canceled. Your team can start bleeding resources as functional managers divert their team members away from this unpromising program to other projects that seem more urgent.

But the effects go beyond your program team. Other teams will be hesitant to try the Rapid Learning Cycles framework. They may even be forbidden to use Agile Development methods because the perception will be that the teams iterate but never reach the end of a program. Rather than demonstrate that Rapid Learning Cycles get products to market faster, you will have demonstrated the opposite.

The Rapid Learning Cycles framework does require more time in the early phases of development—but not twice as much time. I suggest that you start with about 30 percent more time for the phases leading up to Detailed Design—and take that time from the final phases of the program. This will help the team remove some major Knowledge Gaps, and will meet your stakeholders' needs to demonstrate progress toward launch in a reasonable time.

Seven Other Common Speed Bumps and How to Get Over Them

If you avoid the five major failure modes in the previous section, chances are you will be able to sustain the Rapid Learning Cycles framework throughout development. You will have avoided the difficulties that have caused other teams to abandon the framework before it has a chance to get established.

Here are seven more common speed bumps that teams have run into, and how to get over them:

Managers Override Decisions Made by the Team and Don't Use the Team's Accumulated Knowledge

Sometimes the organizational culture supports the idea that managers make all the decisions and product developers just execute them. This is difficult behavior to change. If the people you are dealing with are the ones who invented your company's breakthrough product, they have become very successful by following their past behavior patterns. If you don't deal with this, your team members will soon feel as though the work they put into closing Knowledge Gaps is not valuable, and they will stop making recommendations.

A logical argument to convince the managers to behave differently is probably not going to work. They may or may not agree to change, but in the heat of the moment, they will revert back, sometimes without realizing it. Instead, you need to get them excited about the vision of the product in the hands of customers to connect with the instincts and emotions that drive their decisions.

Then gently kick them out of the Integration Events, in the name of getting this wonderful product out the door as quickly as possible. If these managers need to be involved in making decisions, work with them privately, where it's easier to challenge them to consider the evidence even when it goes against their gut instincts.

Decisions Don't Get Made When They Are Supposed to Be Made According to the Learning Cycles Plan

Sometimes you reach the Last Responsible Moment to make a decision, and it's clear that the team is just not ready. You need to delay the project to give them more time. But this should be the exception. If this happens too often, you will need to dig into it to find out why. Otherwise, it will be impossible to predict when your product will be ready.

If your team doesn't have a compelling reason other than your own desire to get the product out faster, the team may not have enough urgency to overcome its caution. Beef up the urgency by making the final deadline more visible and a bit more aggressive. If at all possible, tie the target launch date to something compelling—a trade show or a major customer visit—that can generate some pull to get it done on time. I worked with one team that tied a percentage of the team's bonus to the final product launch date.

Some organizations have a lot of risk aversion, and they will try to close every Knowledge Gap perfectly before making decisions. You can help the team overcome that tendency by reinforcing the need to make decisions when it is time to make them. It also helps to track the unclosed Knowledge Gaps as risks so that team members know that their concerns are not being dismissed to fit the schedule.

You can model this by assigning yourself ownership for some early Key Decisions that you make at the Last Responsible Moment—not earlier and not later. It's helpful to remind people of the decisions that are coming up, so that they are prepared to make them when they walk into the Integration Event. This means that some people may need to see the Knowledge Gap reports a day or two in advance so that they have time to think ahead of the meeting.

Knowledge Gaps Are Too Large—Nothing Can Be Closed in a Single Learning Cycle

If you reach the first Learning Cycle Event and have not closed any Knowledge Gaps, I suggest that you break the Knowledge Gaps down into smaller ones that have more focus. It's exciting and fun to close Knowledge Gaps. The team needs to have that experience of accomplishment at every event. If more than one event goes by with no closed Knowledge Gaps, the team will start to feel like the program is dragging.

It could also be true that your cadence is too fast. Here's how to tell the difference: if most of your Knowledge Gaps for the first event are almost but not quite closed, consider adding one or two more weeks to the next cycle—without changing the plan. If more Knowledge Gaps close at the next event, (the ones that should have closed this cycle plus the ones for the next cycle), revise the Learning Cycles Plan to reflect this new cadence.

If you still have only a few Knowledge Gaps that close in one learning cycle at the next event, or if this event has a lot of Knowledge Gaps that are not close to being closed, spend some dedicated time breaking the Knowledge Gaps into smaller pieces that do fit within a single learning cycle. You may also need to see if the team has taken on too many things and, if so, remove some that are less important.

Virtual Planning Boards Are Not Visible or Not Updated Frequently

It's possible to run the Learning Cycles Plan virtually, but it does require more maintenance, and the updates need to get back to the team within 24 hours of the meeting. It's too easy for someone on the team to get off track if the plan is not visible when it is needed. You are the busiest person on the team, and if you get behind with this, it will be difficult to get caught up. If you can't delegate these updates to someone else, you need to book time in your calendar to make the updates immediately following every event.

Use simple tools. PowerPoint is fine for creating a simple Virtual Learning Cycles Plan that you can print out on a plotter to hang in the team room, or post as a PDF on a website. People can zoom out to see the big picture and zoom in to see the detail. It will probably not project well, but it does display well on a large screen that is hung so that people can get close to it. You can print it out and hang it on the wall for your events, while the team uses more sticky notes to make changes. This is so much faster and less frustrating than trying to project the plan and then update it.

The purpose-built tools for doing virtual visual planning are getting better, but as of January 2017, I've seen few tools that out-perform a simple grid with rectangles for sticky notes. A virtual version is a challenging technical problem to solve, since it requires integration with smart board vendors' systems and corporate web conferencing solutions.

It's currently impossible for multiple small groups to work on the same plan during a Learning Cycle Event, since there is only one keyboard and one display. It ends up being a lot more work for you to keep the plan updated. For this reason, I still recommend simple tools as the best way to make sure that the Virtual Visual Plan gets updated.

Learning Cycle Event Presentations Go on for Too Long or Have Too Much Data Captured in Slide Sets

I've covered this topic already in a number of different places, but it's here because it is such a common problem. In most companies of any size, in universities and research labs, information gets presented in slide sets. I certainly learned early in my career that I needed to make good slide sets in order to get my ideas heard, and that often these slide sets would be reviewed when I was not there to explain them. Sometimes it seems as though management consulting firms get paid by the slide when they make their recommendations, and I have to admit that I was guilty of this myself before I learned better. I can appreciate how difficult it is to give a presentation backed by a single slide, or a one-page report.

Edward Tufte of Yale University has demonstrated that those slides get in the way of good decisions. We don't remember what was on slide 10 when we are on slide 15. The information is presented as a linear series, when we just want to see the numbers that are important to us. We read faster than anyone can talk. The most important information gets buried as sub-bullets in a sea of text. It's too easy to misinterpret presentations when the presenter is not there to explain them.

It's no wonder that many managers cannot sit through a presentation without interrupting it, causing the presenter to skip ahead to the data that will answer the managers' questions. Such presentations get in the way of good decision making and knowledge sharing. They drag out the events and make them more tedious for the team. The reports don't capture the knowledge that the team has built, making it more difficult to bring that knowledge to bear on decisions.

As the Program Leader, you are responsible for setting a good example early, and for coaching people. You can ask new team members to review their reports with you ahead of the Learning Cycle Event and provide one-on-one coaching to people who are struggling. The first two events are the most challenging, but if you are diligent about maintaining your standards, the team should catch on quickly.

Team Members and/or Stakeholders Keep Asking for a Detailed Project Plan or Gantt Chart

This is another old habit that dies hard. If most program teams have made detailed schedules that specify all the team's activities and deliverables, the team and your stakeholders will expect one from you. You could comply with this request, but it will come at the cost of the time you have available to work with team members on important stuff—Knowledge Gaps and Key Decisions. More important, it puts all the responsibility on you to define the right activities and deliverables for Knowledge Gaps that you have delegated to others.

Instead, push back on team members and encourage them make their own Activity Plans, offering to coach them but not to create the plan for them. In early development, the Learning Cycles Plan should have everything team members need. In later stages, there will be other deliverables to produce, but it's not as though any of them are surprises or require special knowledge that only you have. It's far better for team members to work from their own plan. You can review their plans to make sure they have not missed anything.

I suggest that you take stakeholders on a tour of the program, starting with the Major Milestones Plan and ending with the Learning Cycles Plan. If you have a team that's done an especially good Activity Plan, you can include that too. When stakeholders ask for a detailed plan, they want to know that you are on top of the program and have not missed anything. It will be helpful for them to see that you are getting the benefits of a detailed plan—just in a different way. As a last resort, ask your sponsor for help deflecting the request.

Team Members Don't Challenge Knowledge Gaps or Activities -They Just Do What's on the Plan

If your team members include a lot of junior engineers or people who have not been encouraged to think independently, they may have difficulty with the concept of learning vs. doing. They may need a lot of help building their Activity Plan. Then they will execute the plan, even if something has changed or an opportunity has arisen that should change the direction of their experimentation. Instead, they need to be aware of how their activities contribute to closing Knowledge Gaps, and should stop immediately if it's clear to them that there is no longer any value in the activity.

This situation is best dealt with by working one on one with those who need more encouragement. If there are too many for you to handle yourself, you can assign mentors who can review their work in light of the needs of the overall program. With people who are more timid, it's especially important to support them in developing and executing their own plans, rather than giving in to the temptation to just do it for them. They won't always do exactly what you would do, but that's part of their learning process.

If Your Rapid Learning Cycles Program Goes Off Track

What do you do if you notice that something's not quite right? While I can't outline every possible solution to every challenge that might arise, I can give you the general approach to follow when it seems as though the Rapid Learning Cycles framework is not fitting as well as it could.

Do a Quick Reflection on the Problem:

Find a quiet place away from the team area and away from your own desk, unless you can close the door or put on headphones to avoid interruptions. Use whatever tools help you express your thoughts most easily: paper or laptop. Sit for a moment and think about the situation as you ask yourself these questions:

What do I observe? What do you see, hear or read that's leading to the impression that things are not going as well as they could?

What's going well? What is the team doing right? Where are they succeeding? What should they be encouraged to do even more?

What needs to be improved? What opportunities are there for the team to get better? You can reread the relevant sections of the book to check for mismatches between our recommendations and the team's implementation. Perhaps the team has misinterpreted something or has made an adaptation that doesn't fit.

What should they stop doing? They may have added something to the method that doesn't fit or brought a behavior from other teams that doesn't mesh well with the framework.

What do you need to do next? What actions need to be done in the next few days to implement the ideas that came out of this session?

You can do all of this in fifteen minutes' of quiet time before the next Learning Cycle Event to bring clarity to the situation.

Make an Intervention During the Appropriate Event

Unless things have come to a complete standstill, wait until the next event before changing anything. Issues with the Status Event itself or a team's Activity Plan should be dealt with immediately, but most of the problems can wait until the next Learning Cycle Event. During the team's reflection time, bring up the issue and the change you recommend, and get their agreement to execute it.

Communicate the change to those affected before implementing it. For example, you may find that only some members of the team give lengthy updates, while others stick to the format. Coach these individuals privately before announcing to the entire group that you will be stricter about reinforcing the Status Event structure. If you have stakeholders who just don't seem to understand the concept of the Last Responsible Moment, you'll need to work with them one on one.

Monitor the Changes to See If They Have Made a Difference

Close the loop on your actions. How have your observations changed?

In the early days of developing this framework, we had teams that abandoned it because it just wasn't working for them. We learned from those experiences to build a stronger, more robust framework.

If you have tried to use the framework for at least three Integration Events and it's just not working, it's OK to stop. Perhaps your organization has some major cultural barriers, or your product is ill-suited to the framework for some reason we haven't yet seen in the broader community. You can always contact us for help through the Rapid Learning Cycles Resource Center (see Appendix D).

Even if you have a complete failure of the framework, your program is still better off than it would have been had you followed the normal process. You know a lot more about the risks that you face, and you can still do a lot to close Knowledge Gaps related to Key Decisions that are yet to be made, or that have a high risk of needing to be revisited later.

But failure isn't likely if you've avoided the major problems and adjusted for the rest. The framework is intentionally forgiving. Here are the areas where a lot of different solutions have all proven to be workable.

Areas with Freedom to Create Your Own Solutions

These are the areas where there are many right answers and no one best answer. You can experiment with different approaches with little impact to the program team, until you settle on something you like. Some of these areas may surprise you.

The Cadence of Learning Cycles

Throughout this book, I've described the learning cycle cadence as the "heartbeat" of the program and touted the benefits of giving the team a steady rhythm as the organizing principle for the program. If you change the cadence too often or, worse, delay events just because you don't feel ready, the team will lose the coordinating effects of cadence.

However, it doesn't matter all that much what cadence you set. Some groups like pushing themselves to move fast, and set a cadence that is intentionally uncomfortable. Other groups want to run at a pace that's more relaxed and allows everyone to go home on time to their families. The first team will get more learning done faster than the second team, but the second team will also be much faster than a team that uses a traditional PDP. In fact, some efficiency research shows that a strict 40-hour work week is the best way to maximize effectiveness in the long run.

I recommend that you establish a cadence that feels just a little fast—as if you were going at a brisk walk, not a slow ramble or an all-out sprint. This creates enough urgency to drive creative solutions for closing Knowledge Gaps—but not so much that the team is constantly stressed out. Only you can decide whether four weeks is a cadence you can keep, and it may take some experimentation to find just the right pace.

It also doesn't matter that much if you change the cadence—as long as you do it at Learning Cycle or Integration Events, after reflecting on the team's progress and reviewing the plans. It's helpful to hold it steady for at least three cycles before changing it again. Our hearts have the ability to speed up or slow down in response to our cells' need for oxygen, and your program team can also speed up or slow down in response to the team's capacity and need for learning.

The Frequency of Status Events

Daily, twice a week, weekly or even biweekly Status Events all work, as long as the standup protocol is followed and people are still able to answer the "What have I done?" and "What will I do?" questions with short answers. If you as the Program Leader are not getting many requests for help in between the meetings, the cadence is fast enough.

Since Status Events don't contribute to the team's learning, you may even want to experiment with fewer of them until it's clear that too many problems are cropping up between meetings. Gradual change is best here: add one between events if you need more, and drop every other event if you need fewer. It is important to maintain the synchronization between Learning Cycle Events and Status Events. If you have an odd number of weeks in your learning cycles, you'll need to have Status Events at least weekly or they will get out of sync.

On large teams, subteams may use different cadences for their Status Events, as long as they sync up with Learning Cycle Events. Often the Software group wants to meet every day, but the Mechanical team wants to meet only once a week. That should be OK.

The Method Used to Close Knowledge Gaps

It doesn't matter which variant of the Scientific Method you use to close Knowledge Gaps, as long as it is consistently applied across the entire team. I prefer Design–Experiment–Capture because it was tailored for this kind of work, but if the team has already been trained on a different method, feel free to use it. The main objective is to make sure the team uses the same vocabulary to describe the different stages of closing a Knowledge Gap. When someone says, "I spent some time designing the tests for the competitive analysis today," it should be clear to everyone that he was laying the groundwork for good data collection and analysis.

This is easier if the templates for Knowledge Gap and Key Decision Reports reinforce the method and the vocabulary. A good report template will make it clear that the researcher followed the method, and will make it obvious when one step was missed or rushed through. Since the entire purpose of the framework is to help the team learn what it needs to learn, team members need to hold each other accountable for doing good groundwork before rushing into solution mode. As the Program Leader, you will spend a lot of time working with team members on the best way to use the method to close their Knowledge Gaps.

I would avoid using problem-solving methods designed for process improvement (Improvement Kata, PDCA, 8D, DMAIC—don't worry if you don't know what these are). They need heavy adaptation to fit into the Rapid Learning Cycles framework, and some of them don't scale down very well to address small Knowledge Gaps.

The Approach to Phase Gate Integration

There are many different options for integrating Rapid Learning Cycles into a phase gate process with Gate Reviews. You can combine gates with Integration Events, or you can hold Gate Review meetings either before or after Integration Events. The Gate Reviews can also be completely disconnected as long as they are focused on the business case and not on technical details, and as long as Gate Review participants also attend Integration Events as needed.

Teams normally make a Learning Cycles Plan that covers the time within a phase, but in early development, it might make more sense to make a plan that covers the first two or three phases if they are short.

The Format for Integration Events

There are lots of different ways to hold Integration Events. Most groups start out with Integration Events that look a lot like Learning Cycle Events, except that there are more people and the focus is on Key Decisions. As the product gets more mature, it's helpful to conduct the Integration Event around the product itself: demonstrate the software, have prototypes in the room to play with, pass around components when they're being discussed. It makes the product more tangible, which makes it easier to get good decisions.

As long as the decisions get made and the Learning Cycles Plan gets updated, you can structure the agenda in any way that you like. Some groups like to do a stakeholder review in the morning and a team planning session in the afternoon. Some groups report on all the Knowledge Gaps, and then focus on Key Decisions. Others report on Knowledge Gaps as the team walks through the Key Decisions to be made. The specifics of the agenda matter less than having an agenda and then sticking to it, so that the team can get all the way through the Learning Cycles Plan update.

If the program is going well, it's an exciting event because the team members are eager to share their progress with the larger group, and the need to make Key Decisions leads to interesting discussions about the vision for the product. If the program is not going well, the event will not be as pleasant, but it will lead to the rich discussion that the team needs in order to decide where to go next. The Integration Event provides a container for these conversations, and the shape of the container doesn't matter all that much.

Don't Just Break the Rules— Make Your Own

I hope that you can see by now that innovators have to make their own rules.

If you are in an established R&D organization, you have to be willing to break the rules of your company's Product Development Process (PDP), which encourages making decisions too early, discourages learning early and requires too much unnecessary documentation and too many checklist items.

But long experience in the innovation space shows that teams cannot function in a corporate environment with no rules at all. It sounds like a great idea to throw out everything when a team needs to do something radically different, and it does feel liberating to toss the PDP rule book in the recycling bin. But in practice, teams that throw out the rules without replacing them get bogged down. They suffer from avoidable mistakes, miscommunication and uncoordinated activity that ultimately detract from their ability to make an impact on the company's future.

If you are an entrepreneur, you have no rules to follow—which is both good and bad. Good because you don't have to follow any rules that don't make sense, and bad because some of the traditional rules do lead to better products. But if you don't make your own rules, your partners—channel partners, manufacturing partners, distribution partners and investors—will make rules for you.

Innovative teams of any size don't need rigid rules, but they do need flexible guidelines and frameworks that help them maximize the value of the time and money they have to invest in innovation.

The Rapid Learning Cycles Framework Is a Good Place to Start

If you are burning with the need to bring your vision to life, you may not want to spend any more time thinking about process than you need to get the program running. If you don't want to expend any effort on defining your own rules, you can use this book and the online reference materials as a step-by-step recipe to bring an innovation from idea to launch. After you have been through a few cycles, you will naturally begin to adapt the process so that it fits you better.

If you want to make some changes to your company's PDP to make it more innovation friendly, by now you have a lot of different ideas that you can try out. If you think the PDP is completely broken, you have a proven method to replace it—one that balances your company's need for structure with the freedom you need for innovation.

The Right Balance of Structure and Freedom

Different innovation models have different balance points that depend upon the company's tolerance for risk and the customer's tolerance for immaturity.

You know your product and your development environment better than anyone else. You know how much freedom you have to break your company's rules—or how much structure your startup team will accept if it makes their dreams more likely to come true. You know how fast your market is moving and how forgiving your customers can be about early releases with quality issues. You know how much technology you can leverage, and what you have to build yourself. You are in the best position to define your team's framework so that you can lead the team on the path between you and your new product.

Customers' expectations are different for a new game app vs. a new baby monitor app or a new infant car seat design. Established companies have repeat customers to support, shareholders to satisfy and brand promises to fulfill. Entrepreneurs can take more risks, but that's no excuse for taking dumb risks that cause unnecessary failures. All you learn from those types of failures is that some rules are not made to be broken.

Fail for the Right Reasons

Innovators learn a lot from failure. It could be that your product vision is just not workable. It could require violating the laws of physics or entangling yourself in lawsuits. The customers may not behave in the way you expect when they interact with your product. If your product fails, you want it to fail because the idea itself had some fundamental flaw—you can learn from that to create something new.

You don't want your product to fail from poor execution. I read a case study in a book on innovation about a product that I was salivating to get. It solved a problem that I deal with every day. But when I looked for the product, I found out that it had been pulled from the market—not because there was no market for it or because customers didn't like the idea.

It failed because the execution of the product was so poor that people didn't trust it to work. It was clunky and unreliable, which may be OK for an early adopter market but that's not the market they were in. Customers would stop using it after a few days, and many of them returned it to the company. The quality standards can be lower for a Minimum Viable Product—but they cannot be so low that users don't see the value because of the frustration they experience.

The company was able to raise a lot of money from venture capitalists based upon this great idea. But the product failed due to poor execution. Someday, someone will try again, and this time, they will get the execution right. The new entrepreneurs will capitalize on an opportunity that the original entrepreneurs squandered when they didn't pay enough attention to the fundamentals of product development and customer engagement.

If your product is going to fail, you want it to fail fast, so that you can go on with your life. But you don't want it to fail because you rushed something to market that was too immature for the customers you targeted. You want to know that you did everything possible to succeed as you burn with the desire to see it on the market quickly. You need to find the shortest distance between you and your new product that goes over, around or through the obstacles that can throw your program off track.

The Shortest Distance Between You and Your Product

As an innovator, you make your own trail. But you will get there faster if you save your energy for the parts of your journey where there are no roads to follow.

When the Lewis & Clark Expedition set out to reach the Pacific Ocean from the Midwest in 1804, there was no trail to follow. But they followed waterways and Native American paths, scouting the terrain for the paths of least resistance. They hired Sacagawea, a Native American woman, as a guide and translator to help negotiate with local tribes for support and advice. If they had struck out over land and ignored the advice of the people who already lived there, they wouldn't have made it over the Rocky Mountains. Instead, they made it all the way to the Pacific

Ocean—and back. They lost only one person on the 7,000-mile journey through unmapped terrain.

If your goal is to get your best ideas to market faster, you will be more successful if you don't have to break trail on every aspect of the program. Do you need to innovate on the process too—or can you leverage everything that my clients and I have learned over the past ten years to get your innovations to market faster?

The shortest path between you and your new product is the one that focuses your attention on the aspects of your product that are new and different. That's where the excitement is, that's where the creativity is, and that's where the risks are. A team with clarity about what it knows and what it needs to know is a team that is prepared to get its ideas to market faster.

Get Your Best Ideas to Market Faster

The Rapid Learning Cycles framework is designed to help you get your best ideas to market faster.

It is a forgiving system with a lot of room for personal and team choices. I've showed you where the major bumps are, so that you can steer around them. I've highlighted the areas where you have a lot of freedom to choose and explained how to integrate the framework with the corporate processes that you probably can't completely ignore if you work inside a company. As far as possible, I've given you a recipe to follow, with even more detailed "how-to" instructions online at the book's growing website of resources.

I know you won't follow the recipe exactly.

You can follow the framework as it's given here: work diligently to define Key Decisions and Knowledge Gaps and then ruthlessly prioritize them, and make Key Decisions at the Last Responsible Moment. You can structure your work into learning cycles and keep the event structure but adapt the events so that they fit your team. You can use the framework as inspiration to develop something new. You can supplement with additional rules about good design practices, coding standards and quality expectations.

If you decide to use Rapid Learning Cycles, I can't guarantee success. This is innovation, and the failure rate is high. I can predict that if you do fail, you will fail faster and you will fail for the right reasons, so that you can move on to your next idea having learned everything you can from your experience.

I can predict that when you succeed, you will succeed faster and you will have learned everything you can to extend and repeat your success.

You can get your best ideas to market faster.

APPENDICES

Rapid Learning Cycle Pilot Team Guide

If you are a Program Leader who has decided to use the Rapid Learning Cycles framework for your next program, here is a checklist to help you get started.

How to Use This Book with a Program Team

Here is a step-by-step process for getting your program started with Rapid Learning Cycles:

- Identify the people who will be on your team for the next phase.
- Schedule the date for the Kickoff Event.
- Book the location, ideally off-site but at minimum in a large conference or training room with a lot of wall space. You need extra space for subteams to work in small groups, and a blank wall large enough for your Learning Cycles Plan—even if you will convert it to a virtual plan right after the meeting. The best rooms are square, with space for subteams to sit at square or round tables.

A U-shaped configuration with movable tables is the next best alternative. Small conference rooms with one narrow table don't work very well.

- Ask everyone who will attend the Kickoff Event to read this book before they arrive at the event. It will be helpful (and necessary if you purchased the e-book) for each team member to have his or her own copy of the book. I don't say this to sell more books.

  When team members have questions between events, they need to be able to get back to the source material. They will be able to get their own logins to the Rapid Learning Cycles Resource Center (see Appendix D). If you have more than ten people on your team, you can send a message to me through the site and I can help you with a corporate discount.

- Use the resources available at the Rapid Learning Cycles Resource Center to develop your detailed agenda, outline agenda and supplies list. Make sure you have whatever supplies you need to attach things to the wall in the room you have booked. You may need push-pins, T-pins, masking tape or poster hanging dots.

- Designate a location for your team's Learning Cycles Plan. If it's online, go ahead and download the template at the Resource Center to familiarize yourself with it before the event.

- Customize the templates for the Learning Cycles Plan, Key Decisions Log and Knowledge Gaps Log.

- Purchase supplies. If you have to order them, make sure they will arrive at least a week early in case there are problems.

- Order food and drinks for the lunch and breaks. Teams lose a lot of momentum if they have to go to the company canteen or an outside restaurant for lunch.

- Send an email to the participants a week before the Kickoff Event, reminding them of the need to read the book, but asking them not to prepare or bring anything else.

- Finalize the timings and structure of the final agenda.

- Hold the Kickoff Event.
- IMPORTANT: Post the Learning Cycles Plan in its designated location and post the Knowledge Gaps and Key Decisions logs to the team collaboration site no more than 24 hours after the event.
- Hold your first Status Event as planned, allowing some extra time for adjusting the plan.
- Begin your second Status Event with a reminder of the Status Event rules, then monitor yourself to ensure that you are a good model.

By the third Status Event, your team will be off and running. Plan your first Learning Cycle Event at least two weeks in advance of the date, and then keep going.

APPENDIX B

Book Study Group Guide

Many of my clients have benefited from book study groups to help them make positive changes. They either organized or participated in a book study group that got together regularly to discuss a reading from one of the books available about innovation and product development.

If the idea of Rapid Learning Cycles intrigues you, but you're not sure how the framework would work inside your company, a book study group can help you understand how the framework would need to be modified in order to meet your needs.

For my clients these groups helped create momentum for change, by providing the participants with some time to reflect upon the new ideas they found in their book, and to explore ways that the ideas could help their organization. Often these study groups led to individual experimentation with the practices, and then to pilot groups and ultimately organization-wide programs.

How to Use This Book in a Study Group

Here are the steps to establish a book study group in your company:

- Make a list of people who might join you, then ask them if they would be interested. Look for people who naturally seek to improve how the organization does its work, and who are willing to experiment with new ideas. List more people than you need—at least fifteen.

- Ask them whether or not they would be interested in reading this book as part of a study group. Include a link to the Amazon page for this book, or the supplemental website.

- Once you have at least six people, schedule the first meeting and order the books. If everyone says yes, you may end up with too many for one group. Break it into two or more smaller ones.

- Schedule a conference room that has at least one flip chart for taking notes, and a whiteboard. Chapter reviews should not be so formal that they require a projector.

- At the first meeting, pass out the books, agree upon the meeting schedule, reading assignments, chapter report assignments, group ground rules and expectations. You may decide that the group will keep discussions confidential, will not bring laptops, etc.—set the rules you need to make sure that the meetings stay focused and on track.

- Take action right away if someone misses more than one meeting so that the group doesn't lose momentum. As the organizer, it's your responsibility to check in when people go missing. If the group isn't working for someone, it's better to let him or her go gracefully, so that everyone else is not distracted by the absences.

- After you have finished the book, hold one final meeting to reflect upon the group's experience. They may want to tackle another book, or they may want to take some group action to put the ideas into place.

- Celebrate! Do something special to bring the group to a good conclusion.

Best Practices from My Clients

People who have organized book groups have shared a number of ideas about how to run these groups effectively.

Keep Reading Assignments Short and Focused

There is no way to sugar-coat this: book study groups are extra work. Even if you have a powerfully motivated group, it's important to keep the assignments bite-sized. Not only does that make it easier to get the readings done, it also makes it easier to reflect and internalize the things you learned from the reading as the group discusses them. In this book, one chapter per session will be about right.

Keep Chapter Reports Informal and Discussion-Based

Please don't assign a book report on every chapter. We're not in seventh-grade English class. It is helpful to assign someone to facilitate the study group meetings, but he or she should summarize the main ideas on a flip chart and then generate some discussion questions for the group to consider.

Meet on a Regular Schedule and Commit to Attending Each Meeting

These groups thrive on consistency and a regular cadence of meetings. They can be weekly, every two weeks or monthly, depending upon how

293

intensely the group wants to work together. Being human, some people will read the assignment the day before the meeting no matter how much time there is between them, and others will read the whole book because it's interesting.

These groups fall apart when attendance is inconsistent or people come unprepared. Erratic attendance drains away the group's momentum. Group members need to commit to every meeting unless there is a true emergency or they let group members know in advance that they have a conflict. They need to have done the reading when they arrive.

Keep the Group Small and Closed

These groups help build momentum because they help create strong relationships and a shared base of experience among a group of potential Rapid Learning Cycle Program Leaders. That starts to break down once the group gets larger than twelve, or if group membership changes too often. Close the group to new members after the first three meetings. Larger groups can be broken down into small ones, and latecomers can be encouraged to organize their own.

Do Something Together to Make the New Ideas Actionable

Each meeting can end with the commitment to take action, either individually or as a group. The actions might be to test out one of the ideas from the book, to spend some time observing the organization or to identify and eliminate an obvious source of unnecessary waste. They don't have to be large actions to get the ball rolling. Small ones add up.

After You Finish, What Next?

At the companies I've talked with, book study groups enlisted product development leadership, recruited and supported pilot teams, built and delivered training programs and mentored others in problem-solving skills.

Chances are, your own group will have developed lots of ideas for next steps and will already have begun to experiment with some elements of the Rapid Learning Cycles framework. When you are ready to run a pilot team, someone from this group will be the best prepared to serve as the Program Leader.

I would encourage you to keep the group together as an advisory board to help shape your organization's next steps with the Rapid Learning Cycles framework. The group may not need to meet as often. By now, you should know which members are fully on board and which ones are still skeptical. The enthusiastic supporters keep you going and the skeptics keep you honest.

APPENDIX C

Tools to Support Rapid Learning Cycles

I often get asked about tools—especially the software tools that support the Rapid Learning Cycles framework.

If you are in a corporate R&D environment, you probably have everything you need plus a few things you don't need. In fact you may need to negotiate with some system owners who built their tools based on the assumptions behind traditional product development.

If you are working on your own, there are a few basic things that will help. Even if it's just you in the garage right now, you will need to build a team eventually. If you get used to using these tools now, it will be easier to bring new members on board.

Real-Time Collaboration Tools

These are the tools Rapid Learning Cycles teams use most often, even if the team has global distribution.

- Whiteboards and markers, flip charts, paper, pens, pencils
- Digital camera (phone/tablet camera OK), scanner
- Printer and scanner that can handle A3/Tabloid printing and scanning

The physical tools support real-time, face-to-face collaboration, and the digitizing tools make it possible for you to share such work with remote team members.

Some companies have begun to invest in smart whiteboard systems that allow for whiteboard-style collaboration with remote partners. I've seen a lot of them sit idle because only one or two people know how to use them. These boards can be great resources for your team if you are willing to take the time to master the system.

Online Tools

It's possible to run the Rapid Learning Cycles framework with a simple file share. As long as all team members can get to the same location on the server or in the cloud, this is a perfectly good way to collaborate. But a robust collaboration tool gives the team a lot more options.

Collaboration Tools

Collaboration tools such as Microsoft's SharePoint and OneNote or cloud-based collaboration systems such as Basecamp provide the team with a website where they can post documents. Revision control keeps track of the latest versions of key documents. Search functionality makes it easier to find them.

Teams can keep their Key Decision and Knowledge Gap Logs in these tools, then link the Key Decision and Knowledge Gap Reports to these records. This makes it easy to navigate among these reports during Learning Cycle and Integration Events.

These tools have the ability to store metadata about documents, such as Revision Date, Author and Keywords that make it easier to leverage the knowledge that they contain.

Product Data Management and Configuration Management Systems

Occasionally, I find someone working in an entrepreneurial setting without basic tools to track product knowledge. For software, Configuration Management Systems maintain the official versions of software in development. Check in and check out functions provide both conflict avoidance and traceability. Branch paths support iterative development.

Product Data Management Systems do the same thing for hardware. They manage the Bill of Materials (BOM), keep track of supplier agreements and key communications, support workflows for reviewing and approving drawings and process diagrams and provide a home for complicated models.

Most corporate R&D groups already have tools like this, but they are often lacking in small companies because they used to be cost-prohibitive. Today, there are some good cloud-based solutions out there that are appropriately scaled for the entrepreneurial team. This should be something that you have and use, but not something that you have to spend a lot of time maintaining.

Knowledge Supermarket Systems

An ideal Knowledge Supermarket would keep track of a few key pieces of metadata about each knowledge capture document, without restricting the format of the document itself. Rapid Learning Cycles teams use Knowledge Gap and Key Decision reports to capture their knowledge.

The system should be able to accept these reports as they are, asking only for the metadata required to properly categorize them.

A good Knowledge Supermarket would allow for both browsing by topic and searching by keywords. Full text searches sound great in theory, but provide too many hits in practice. With keywords, the author decides when the document shows up in searches—and when it's not relevant.

The website at the Rapid Learning Cycles Resource Center website (http://community.rapidlearningcycles.com) is set up to model an effective Knowledge Supermarket with capacity for as many as 500 documents. When we grow beyond that size, we will need to develop a new user interface to access the materials, but the underlying structure will be sound for at least two more orders of magnitude in content growth.

Tools to Avoid

These tools get in the way of doing Rapid Learning Cycles, because they were built in the old paradigm of traditional product development. If you can't avoid them without violating corporate policy, minimize the amount of time you spend on them and the amount of data you store in them.

- **Requirements Management Systems:** These systems are built around the waterfall paradigm of defining requirements up front and then putting them under heavyweight change control.

  If you must use a system like this, load the requirements into the system as late as possible—the Last Responsible

Moment for making a decision about the requirement. Delay finalizing the requirements as long as possible. If you are measured on this, you will need to get permission to take a different approach, or you will spend way too much time explaining to people why you are not defining requirements before the team is ready to commit to them.

Some groups have adapted their RM systems into places to track Key Decisions and Knowledge Gaps or to store Key Decision and Knowledge Gap reports. They have succeeded by not attempting to replicate the Key Decision and Knowledge Gap Reports with data entry fields inside the system, which makes the reports too difficult to use during events. Instead they used the system to store the report documents with metadata.

- **Knowledge Management Systems:** Most enterprise Knowledge Management systems are too elaborate and complicated to store your team's knowledge. Your team needs to be able to access its knowledge quickly, and control access to it.

The Knowledge Management Systems that we have seen are seriously overbuilt. They have been shown to work in industries that rely upon shared knowledge, primarily large management consulting firms. Those firms may try to sell you a Knowledge Management System, but you probably need a much simpler solution, at least until you have a lot of content to organize.

Your collaboration site is a much better solution when you are at the beginning. Even when a program is finished and you want to share your knowledge with others, the organization's Knowledge Supermarket should be as simple as possible. Scalable collaboration sites should be able to handle your needs until you have more than 1,000 documents to share.

Then you may need a more sophisticated tool but you will also have the knowledge base to help you make a good tool selection and then populate it with the content that will make it a valuable resource right away.

- **Enterprise Project Management Systems:** These systems are dangerous for product development. They give senior managers the illusion of certainty, when the plans they view through such a tool are much more complex and dynamic.

  If you must use such a system, store only your Key Decision sequence in there—keep the Knowledge Gaps and activities out of it. You might choose to keep some of the standard deliverables on the plan if that helps your team remember to do them. The time you would normally spend within this system is time you will spend with your team's Learning Cycles Plan and Activity Plans that change too often to put into a system like this.

Start with What You Have

If this is your first experience with Rapid Learning Cycles, don't buy anything. Don't buy a Virtual Visual Planning System or a smart board. Get waivers so that you can avoid Requirements Management, Knowledge Management or Project Management systems—or at least minimize your contact with them.

Instead, settle on a simple collaboration system that allows the team to share documents as easily as possible. You can probably build this out of the tools you already have or that you can get via cloud-based systems.

Most corporate R&D environments already have some repository to keep product knowledge and software code secure. If you are on your own, this is the one thing to get before you do anything else. If you already have established your repository, and developed good habits for using it, it will be much easier to add new people to your team as you grow.

Until you have some experience, and have begun to adapt the framework to your environment, it will be hard to anticipate your needs so that you can choose the right tools. For Virtual Visual Planning, six months to a year of delay should give you much better alternatives to choose from.

APPENDIX D

How to Learn More About Rapid Learning Cycles

The Rapid Learning Cycles Institute offers a number of opportunities to learn more about the Rapid Learning Cycles framework. We also offer online and in-person learning opportunities for individuals and teams at our main website, http://rapidLearning Cycles.com.

The Rapid Learning Cycles Resource Center

The Rapid Learning Cycles Resource Center offers a number of articles, templates and sample documents for Program Leaders and others who are using the Rapid Learning Cycles framework.

Resource Center members have our permission to download templates, modify them and distribute them to their teams. The other resources on the site may be shared with others, so long as they retain my authorship and copyright notices.

Membership is free in exchange for your permission to send notifications about new content and other learning opportunities.

To join the Rapid Learning Cycles Resource Center, visit
http://community.rapidlearningcycles.com.

Rapid Learning Cycles Video Classes

To go more deeply into the content covered in this book, consider joining one of our video classes. These classes cover the elements of the framework in more detail, and they are a great way to introduce the Rapid Learning Cycles framework to a group that is interested in exploring the it.

They are tailored for those who want to evaluate the Rapid Learning Cycles framework to see if their organization should sponsor a pilot program, and for those who will be participating on teams that will use the Rapid Learning Cycles framework.

We offer individual and site licenses for our video series to encourage teams to watch the videos and discuss the ideas together.

Rapid Learning Cycles Certification Workshops

When you are ready to use the Rapid Learning Cycles framework for the first time, consider taking a Rapid Learning Cycles Program Managers Certification Workshop.

This two-day learning experience is intended to prepare you to run a Kickoff Event for a team, assist the team as it goes through learning cycles, and then run Learning Cycle and Integration Events.

Upon completion of this workshop and the other certification requirements, you will attain the Rapid Learning Cycles Certified™ Program Manager designation. This grants access to a library of reusable presentations, templates and planning guides that will help you use the Rapid Learning Cycles framework with your teams. These are the same materials we have used with our own clients.

You also receive a membership in the Rapid Learning Cycles Certified™ Professionals Community, with discussion forums, advanced content and regular updates to the Rapid Learning Cycles framework documentation.

This is also the first step towards becoming a Rapid Learning Cycles Certified™ Facilitator, which grants expanded access and customization rights, and as well as access to our certified coach and consultant programs for external consultants and trainers.

The Rapid Learning Cycles Institute offers this workshop in many locations around the world directly and through our network of Rapid Learning Cycles Certified™ Consultants.

To learn more about these, go to
http://rapidlearningcycles.com.

Acknowledgments

My gratitude goes first to my clients and colleagues, who have helped me develop and sharpen the Rapid Learning Cycles framework over the past ten years. I have appreciated the opportunity to watch so many great products come to life, and to learn from each and every one of you.

Among the many, special recognition goes to Kathy Iberle, Tim Schipper, Roger Johnson, Carsten Lauridsen, Tine Jørgensen, Suzanne van Egmond, Michael Naughton and Rich Gildersleeve, who all contributed to the evolution of the key framework elements.

I also want to thank the members of the Lean Product Development Resource Center, who have participated in the conversation, sometimes by arguing with me via email. This book would not be nearly as complete without the invaluable feedback from my volunteer pre-readers who gave me detailed notes on improvement opportunities, large and small.

The Lean Product & Process Development Exchange gave me many opportunities to test out my teaching methods with diverse audiences. Thanks to Board Chair Jorrit De Groot, and Board Members Bella Englebach, Ron Marsiglio, Peter Palmer, Jim Morgan, Flemming Moss and Dr. Göran Gustafsson.

Finally, thanks to my husband and business partner, Gene Radeka, for thorough and detailed editing of my earliest drafts to shape the material into a coherent framework, for supporting my clients and me in a thousand different visible and invisible ways, and for being my traveling companion, sounding board, strategic analyst and best friend on this journey.

About the Author

Katherine Radeka

Katherine Radeka has a rare combination of business acumen, scientific depth and ability to untangle the organizational knots to remove the barriers to change. Since 2005, Whittier Consulting Group, Inc. has helped some of the world's leading companies get their products to market faster. She has a global reach with clients in Europe, North and South America, Asia, and Australia/New Zealand.

Katherine is the author of the Shingo Research Award winning book *The Mastery of Innovation: A Field Guide to Lean Product Development.* This book contains 19 case studies of companies who have used lean product development to get their ideas to market faster.

She has published over 200 articles at the Lean Product Development Resource Center and in other venues, including AME's Target Magazine, PDMA's Visions, the Journal for Product Innovation Management, and Real Innovation.

In 2007, she co-founded the Lean Product & Process Development Exchange with Durward Sobek. The organization conducts two conferences per year, one in Europe and one in North America, focused on the principles and practices of Lean Product Development.

Katherine has climbed seven of the tallest peaks in the Cascade Mountains and spent ten days alone on the Pacific Crest Trail, until an encounter with a bear convinced her that she needed a change in strategic direction.

Index

L

Register This Book

Register your copy of this book to receive access to resources that will help you experiment with the ideas in this book. We keep these resources in a special Readers section of the Rapid Learning Cycles Resource Center, accessible through the "Register My Book" link at this URL:

http://community.rapidlearningcycles.com/register-book

Benefits of Registration:

- Templates for Key Decision Reports, Knowledge Gap Reports and Key Decision / Knowledge Gap Logs that may be adapted and distributed to your teams, in a variety of formats.
- Distributable glossary of Key Terms in this book.
- Extended Book Study Guide for teams—and also helpful for individuals who are reading the book on their own.

If you purchased your copy of this book through the Rapid Learning Cycles Institute, or received a copy as part of a workshop or online class sponsored by the Institute, then we have registered the book for you.

If you purchased an eBook, received a softcover book as part of a company purchase or at a public event, or purchased a softcover book from a distribution partner, then you will need to register the book yourself.

Registration Instructions

Use the Register My Book form at the web site to notify us that you need to register your copy of this book. We'll reply back with a link to the resources within one business day, after verifying your purchase.

CPSIA information can be obtained
at www.ICGtesting.com
Printed in the USA
FSHW010042130220
66918FS